D0498138

WITHDRAWN
UTSA LIBRARIES

REGIONAL CONFLICT
AND
NATIONAL POLICY

Contributors

Emery N. Castle
Allen V. Kneese
Hans H. Landsberg
Kent A. Price
Nathan Rosenberg
Clifford S. Russell
Richard B. Stewart
Paul E. Tsongas
Gilbert F. White

REGIONAL CONFLICT AND NATIONAL POLICY

edited by
KENT A. PRICE

LIBRARY
The University of Texas
At San Antonio

Published by Resources for the Future, Inc.
Washington, D.C.
Distributed by The Johns Hopkins University Press
Baltimore and London

Copyright © 1982 by Resources for the Future, Inc.
All rights reserved
Manufactured in the United States of America

Published by Resources for the Future, Inc., 1755 Massachusetts Avenue, N.W.,
Washington, D.C. 20036.
Distributed by The Johns Hopkins University Press, Baltimore, Maryland 21218;
The Johns Hopkins Press Ltd., London.

Library of Congress Cataloging in Publication Data
Main entry under title:

Regional conflict and national policy

  Includes bibliographical references and index.
  1. Natural resources—Government policy—United
States.   2. United States—Economic conditions—
1971–   —Regional disparities.   3. United States
—Economic policy—1981–   4. Energy Policy—
United States.   I. Price, Kent A.
HC103.7.R36   1982   333.7'0973   82-47983
ISBN 0-8018-2918-6
ISBN 0-8018-2919-4 (pbk.)

RESOURCES FOR THE FUTURE, INC.
1755 Massachusetts Avenue, N.W., Washington, D.C. 20036

DIRECTORS

M. Gordon Wolman, *Chairman*
Charles E. Bishop
Roberto de O. Campos
Anne P. Carter
Emery N. Castle
William T. Creson
Jerry D. Geist
David S. R. Leighton
Franklin A. Lindsay
George C. McGhee

Vincent E. McKelvey
Richard W. Manderbach
Laurence I. Moss
Mrs. Oscar M. Ruebhausen
Leopoldo Solís
Janez Stanovnik
Carl H. Stoltenberg
Russell E. Train
Robert M. White
Franklin H. Williams

HONORARY DIRECTORS

Horace M. Albright
Edward J. Cleary
Hugh L. Keenleyside

Edward S. Mason
William S. Paley
John W Vanderwilt

OFFICERS

Emery N. Castle, *President*
Edward F. Hand, *Secretary-Treasurer*

Resources for the Future is a nonprofit organization for research and education in the development, conservation, and use of natural resources, including the quality of the environment. It was established in 1952 with the cooperation of the Ford Foundation. Grants for research are accepted from government and private sources only on the condition that RFF shall be solely responsible for the conduct of the research and free to make its results available to the public. Most of the work of Resources for the Future is carried out by its resident staff; part is supported by grants to universities and other nonprofit organizations. Unless otherwise stated, interpretations and conclusions in RFF publications are those of the authors; the organization takes responsibility for the selection of significant subjects for study, the competence of the researchers, and their freedom of inquiry.

This book was edited by Jo Hinkel and designed by Elsa B. Williams. The index was prepared by John F. Holman & Co. Inc.

Contents

Foreword by Paul E. Tsongas   xi

Preface by Emery N. Castle   xv

chapter one
Introduction and Overview   *Kent A. Price*   1

The Notion of Region   2
Regional Conflict   4
History and Perspective   5
Energy "Haves" and "Have-Nots"   6
Typical Cases Involving Natural Resources   8
Legal Structure of Interstate Resource Conflicts   9
Externality, Conflict, and Decision   10
Epilogue   11
Conclusions   12
Notes   17

chapter two
History and Perspective   *Nathan Rosenberg*   18

The Frontier Thesis   19
Changing Times   20
Environmental Equity   21
Regional Specialization   23
Regional Convergence   26
Equity's Threat to Positive Change   29
Meeting the Policy Test   31
Notes   33

chapter three
Energy "Haves" and "Have-Nots"
Hans H. Landsberg   34

Eastern and Western Coal   35
Coal Slurry Pipelines   38
Severance and Other Local Taxes   41
Population Movements   45
Shifts in Per Capita Income   46
Differential Impact on Consumers   49
How Serious a Problem?   56
Notes   58

chapter four
Typical Cases Involving Natural Resources
Allen V. Kneese   59

Salinity in the Colorado River   60
The Montana Coal Tax   67
The Waste Isolation Pilot Plant Controversy   75
Notes   85

chapter five
The Legal Structure of Interstate Resource
Conflicts   *Richard B. Stewart*   87

Framing the Constitution   89
Origins of Commerce Power   90

Regulation and Taxation of Natural Resources 92
Explaining Judicial Deference 95
Congressional Powers 98
Transboundary Nonmarket Impacts 101
Dialectical Federalism 105
Notes 106

chapter six
Externality, Conflict, and Decision
Clifford S. Russell 110

Three Kinds of Externality 111
Pecuniary Externalities 113
Real Externalities 116
Political Externalities 119
New Approaches 120
Notes 123

Epilogue *Gilbert F. White* 126

What Are Regional Conflicts? 127
The Record of Collective Decision Making 129
National Policy Prospects 130

About the Contributors 133

Index 137

Tables and Figures

Tables

2-1 Personal Income Per Capita in Each Region as Percentage of
     U.S. Average, 1840–1950   27
2-2 Regional Per Capita Income as Percentage of U.S. Average,
     for Selected Years, 1900–77   28

3-1   U.S. Coal Production, East and West of the Mississippi River,
      1950–80   36
3-2   State Production Taxes on Coal, Oil, Natural Gas, as of 1979   42
3-3   Severance Tax Revenues for Selected States, 1979   43
3-4   Yearly Percentage of Population Growth by Region, 1940–80   45
3-5   Average Prices of Residential Energy Sources Delivered to
      User—Nationwide and by Census Region, April 1978–March
      1979   51
3-6   Average Energy Prices, by Region, for 1970 and 1980   53
3-7   Residential Energy Expenditures Per Household, for 1970 and
      1980   54

Figures

1-1   "My Section of the Country, Right or Wrong!"   3

3-1   Geographic Center of U.S. Population, 1790–1980   46
3-2   Regional Per Capita Income as Percentage of U.S. Average,
      1929–79   48
3-3   Relative Per Capita Income in Selected Energy-Surplus and
      Energy-Deficient States, 1929–79   50

Foreword

The issues of conservation, the environment, and energy have enormous implications not only in terms of those issues specifically, but also for regional conflict in the United States. If we are to have any kind of resolution of these issues, there must be a sense of equity, that everyone is sacrificing equally. If there is a perception of inequity, then all of the ingredients are there for social unrest.

Resource Reality

I think a major generator of regional problems is that oil is a finite diminishing resource. That is a reality around which everything else revolves. Politically, the Republicans would argue production, production, production—that the way out of the dilemma of a finite diminishing resource is to produce it faster. My understanding of resource management is that when you have something that is diminishing, you try to husband it and rely more on things that are inexhaustible. A production scenario is a drain-America-first approach. That may be all right for us, but can we defend that point with our grandchildren?

The Democrats, on the other hand, will tell you that the energy crisis is a function of the oil companies—that somehow if you could put Mary Poppins at the head of Exxon the problems would go away.

Both of these approaches are equally absurd, equally rhetorical, and equally successful. When talking to the convinced, they are very powerful. And that is basically how most people address the issue: we are awash in rhetoric, not to mention hypocrisy, when what we need is a careful sorting and weighing of the facts and values involved in making—or not making—a decision.

For example, a contentious issue in the Northeast is offshore drilling on Georges Bank. Oil does exist there, but apparently only in limited amounts, and its development has serious implications both for the fishery resource and for tourism. The exploration and production of that oil therefore must be done in a way that recognizes the regional needs for tourism and fishery development to remain intact.

Let me use two examples about how this plays itself out in the real political world. The 1980 Alaska lands bill offered a classic example of confrontation between regional interests and what is perceived to be the national good. Those who wanted a more development-oriented Alaska lands bill argued, in effect, that "this is our land and we'll do what we want with it." Those on the other side argued that much of Alaska was federal land—national parks, wildlife refuges, and wilderness that basically belong to everybody—and that this national interest had to be considered.

The debate came down to a question of where national interest overrides regional interest, and I chose the national side. Of course, in this instance I had the luxury of representing an area far from that under contention. To be truthful, had I been a senator from Alaska, I might well have voted the other way. Parochial voting patterns aside, however, I think it does make a difference what form an assertion of national interest takes. In the case of Georges Bank, the purported national interest might well be destructive. For the Alaska lands, it is conserving. The former could be irreversible, while the latter preserves both land and options for the future.

Another personal example. In 1980 I put forth the "Massachusetts Plan," which outlined what our regional response as a state should be to the energy dilemma. It involved over 250 recommendations that covered every conceivable area to, in essence, insulate Massachusetts from the inevitable shocks in terms of both the price of oil and its supply over time.

The Massachusetts Plan probably was the best thing that we have done in our office, but it was received with a giant yawn. It made page 21 of the *Boston Globe*, page 6 of the *Boston Herald American,* was covered in all the other regional papers and has not been heard of since.

What happened here? Basically, I think we overwhelmed the media and the political process by the sheer number and complexity of our recommendations. And I think we probably erred in not setting priorities among them. The Massachusetts Plan just did not make it in the world of political reality and no amount of frustration on our part could change that reality.

An Era of Conflict

As the chapters that follow make abundantly clear, the United States is well into another one of those times characterized by complex issues that involve a potential for conflict between, for example, coal-producing states that want to impose a severance tax and those of us who are going to have to pay that tax, between areas that bear the brunt of strip mining for coal and states that want to convert it into electricity, between oil-producing and oil-consuming states. In good times, when everybody is doing well and the economic pie is expanding, these kinds of regional differences do not have much impact. But in a time such as we have now—when the pie is not expanding but indeed is contracting—there is a much more heightened sensitivity to perceived inequity, that someone else may be getting away with something that hurts us when we are already hurting.

This creates a political climate for taking advantage of that situation and exploiting it. Granted, dealing with this is very difficult, but the way that we are dealing with it in Washington is exactly the opposite of what we should be doing. I believe that the only practical way to solve a conflict between regions is to come over it from the top, which means a federal solution, and that is not the way we are heading. If the Ohio River Valley burns a great deal of coal and one result is increased acid rain in Canada, in New England, and in upstate New York, who is to resolve that? When it is not in the economic interest of Ohio to do it, but it is in the interest of everyone else downwind, who but the federal government can come in and resolve that problem?

The current notion that there is little or no role for the federal government is simply a swing of the pendulum, the country having rejected as unworkable—and, I think, rightly so—the prior notion that government should be in everything. The pendulum has gone past center and is going up the other side, but in time that also will peak and we will come down to an era where the issue is, How do we do it, How will it work?

Let us forget the rhetoric on both sides, and try to ignore, whether problems—or solutions—are labeled Democratic or Republican. I hope for a coming together of both parties in a much more pragmatic, realistic sense.

There are no easy answers, but indeed there are answers. What this volume brings to the debate is some rationality and an approach free of ideology, in which the question is, What works? Not what should work, not what would we like to see work, but indeed, what works?

Washington, D.C.
May 1982

Paul E. Tsongas (D–Mass.)
United States Senate

Preface

In the spring of 1980, at its semiannual meeting, the Board of Directors of Resources for the Future asked me to discuss with the staff the possibility of an annual forum. Specifically, the idea was to select an important resource or environmental topic and explore it in some depth for the benefit of leaders in industry, government, academia, foundations, and eventually the public at large. The primary purpose would not be to offer easy solutions or to debate controversial topics, but rather would be to identify existing or emerging problems and to illuminate them in such a way that subsequent decision making would be improved.

I reported back to the Board in October 1980 with a proposed format and was encouraged to proceed. One of the first tasks—the selection of a topic—was made easier by Kenneth D. Frederick, director of RFF's Renewable Resources Division. His suggestion of "Regional Conflict and National Policy" met all our requirements in terms of substance and was embraced with enthusiasm by those of us involved in planning the event.

But the selection of a topic was just the beginning, especially this particular topic. There is no question of its importance or timely nature. Nearly everyone is familiar with such terms as "the Sagebrush Rebellion" and "the Snowbelt versus the Sunbelt," and with the controversies generated by severance taxes on the extraction of energy resources. The problem was that the examples are so numerous and the conflicts so sharp that we risked achieving few insights beyond those that a well-read person could obtain from the popular press.

Moreover, it is not obvious that problems of regional conflict can be thought about on other than an individual basis. To say the same thing another way, "Are there any principles that can guide us as we consider such problems?"

After considerable study and discussion, we concluded that indeed there are some guiding principles and generalizations that can be used in understanding these problems. One set of generalizations comes from history. After all, regional conflict is not new in the United States; our entire history is replete with examples. While present conflicts may differ in degree or even in level, and although they may require different approaches for solution, it is imprudent to proceed without examining our present difficulties in the context of past regional conflicts.

The other common element is that we have one basic set of institutions to use in our search for solutions. Powers are divided between the federal government and states in a particular way and are exercised through the legislative, judicial, and administrative branches of government. Thus, it seemed to us that regional conflicts should be viewed in the interwoven context of history and the framework provided by our system of government. And from a practical point of view, resolution of regional conflicts is not likely to get very far unless they are viewed in the context of economic history and in a realistic way with respect to the economic, legal, jurisdictional, and political setting.

The forum was presented on October 21, 1981, in Washington, D.C., before a distinguished audience. The program drew on talent from outside as well as inside Resources for the Future. Nathan Rosenberg of Stanford University has been associated with RFF over the years and, knowing of his talents, we turned to him immediately to provide the historical perspective. Our own Hans H. Landsberg and Allen V. Kneese offered contemporary examples of regional conflict, and Harvard's Richard B. Stewart detailed the legal structure within which interstate resource conflicts are contested. RFF's Clifford S. Russell presented a classification of conflict that is helpful in thinking about such problems, but which carries its own share of controversy. And Gilbert F. White, former chairman of the RFF Board, summarized the Forum's contributions in a masterful presentation that was a highlight of the day.

The luncheon speaker was Sen. Paul E. Tsongas, who viewed regional conflict from the standpoint of one who is in the midst of the fray and who must view such problems neither with indifference nor detachment. Excerpts from the senator's extemporaneous remarks appear as the Foreword to this volume.

What follows in a sense are the proceedings of the 1981 Fall Forum. But this is more than a proceedings volume. Some of the chapters are longer and more comprehensive than was possible in an oral presentation, some have been extensively rewritten by their authors since the Forum, and all have been revised and edited by RFF's Kent A. Price, who also has provided an introduction and overview. The result is not a collection of loosely related papers but rather a book—a cohesive, readable, scholarly survey and analysis of a set of troubling issues that badly need dispassionate assessment.

For thirty years Resources for the Future has maintained a policy of strict nonadvocacy: research and objective analysis are our products, rather than policy prescriptions or political positions. Hence, in this book, as in the Forum, the focus is on facts and processes rather than on identifying regional culprits or offering "solutions" to one or another conflict. Our belief is that there are no perfect solutions that can be taken off the shelf and applied effectively; answers and solutions are likely to emerge only after painstaking analysis and consensus development. In the meantime, firms and agencies must make decisions, and it is important that those decisions be approached with the best information available and with realism about the prospects for conflict resolution.

In addition to the authors, three members of RFF's Public Affairs staff contributed importantly to the publication of this book. Patricia M. Parker painstakingly prepared the manuscript for computer typesetting in the first such application of RFF's new computer-word processing equipment. Jo Hinkel checked the manuscript's consistency and accuracy and in general ensured that it met RFF's exacting standards of publication. And Elsa B. Williams designed the volume and oversaw its transformation from manuscript to bound book. These tasks—and the spirit in which they were performed—too often go unsung, but they are of no little consequence and are gratefully acknowledged.

Washington, D.C.
June 1982

Emery N. Castle
President and Senior Fellow
Resources for the Future

chapter one

Introduction and Overview

Kent A. Price

Compare the jumbled national frontiers of Europe with the orderly state borders of the American West. For that matter, compare those of the original thirteen colonies and the other older, eastern states with the neat rectangles and straight lines that predominate west of the Mississippi. There are few straight lines in nature, let alone a nature complicated by human diversity. The conclusion is inescapable that the boundaries of the western states were established more or less arbitrarily.

This is important in the context of conflicts among regions in the United States because many such conflicts now have a distinctly western flavor. Disputes over water and energy resources are not unknown in the rest of the country, for example, but they seem to reach a higher pitch in the West. The Sagebrush Rebellion of course is a purely western phenomenon. And the size, configuration, and location of the western states play parts in these interregional dramas. If Montana were as small as Vermont or as populous as New Jersey, for example, the controversy over its taxation of its coal resources—and the extent of those resources—surely would be very different. Eastern Colorado might well be part of Kansas if its principal activity—wheat farming—were given due weight. Could what is considered the worst-case example of energy boomtowns—Gillette, Wyoming—have happened outside of the sparsely populated, wide-open West? States by no means are inconsequential entities, but their borders frequently are violated by less precisely drawn forces—climate, geography, agriculture, industry, population size and characteristics, resource endowment, and history, to name only the most prominent.

The Notion of Region

Nor do states necessarily capture the feelings and loyalties of their citizens. When I was growing up in the San Francisco Bay Area in the 1950s, the feeling that northern and southern California were two different states (of mind, if not legally) was almost palpable. When a San Francisco radio personality suggested partitioning the state at the Tehachapi Mountains—thus severing Los Angeles—the popular response was enthusiastic. The claims of separateness were many and varied—from climate to culture—but significantly they included water. The north had it and the much more populous south wanted it, and the squabbles over its distribution were and are intense.

I now live in northern Virginia, which the rest of the state justifiably regards as beyond the pale. Never mind that George Washington and George Mason were northern Virginians, nor indeed that Robert E. Lee himself was Alexandria-bred, the area now unmistakably is an extension of Washington, D.C., and thus foreign to those who keep alive the flame of the Old Dominion.

Similarly, New York City long has been viewed with understandable suspicion by upstate New Yorkers. Pensacola and the rest of the Florida Panhandle have much more in common with Alabama than with Miami. Some citizens of the Nebraska Panhandle are talking up secession from that state and affiliation with Wyoming. Not to belabor the point, state lines often seem to be anomalies. Whatever reasons once led to their establishment, in some cases they now are anachronisms.

What Is a Region?

To the extent that states fall short of representing how their inhabitants feel, what they produce, and dozens of other characteristics, the notion

"My section of the country, right or wrong!"

Figure 1–1. Drawing by D. Fradon; © 1979. The New Yorker Magazine, Inc.

of regions perhaps best fills the gap.[1] However intangibly, people clearly do regard themselves as, say, New Englanders, or southerners. But just what is a region?

Interestingly—and significantly for regional disputes—regions do not even exist legally. As Richard B. Stewart points out later in this volume, "States, not regions, are the entities recognized by the law." This is echoed and amplified by Clifford Russell in chapter 6: "Regions lack decision-making institutions and thus are nothing but collections of states, with state decisions and actions defining 'regional' positions."

Yet regions certainly do exist, and the real and potential conflicts among them are so manifest that Resources for the Future deemed the topic worthy of its first major forum in some years. Hence, too, of course, this book. Nathan Rosenberg essays this definition in chapter 2: "loose geographic units larger than a state and smaller than the nation and presumably with some objective characteristic of homogeneity." No one can argue with that, but a greater degree of specificity can elicit disagreement. As Rosenberg says, "Different criteria lead to the identification of very different geographic entities, and most criteria are confronted with continua of variation, with no well-defined, or discrete, boundaries."

Regions are hard to define because the realities they reflect shift with time, perspective, and technological progress. The now immensely productive Great Plains, for example, once were known as the Great American Desert. To a native Californian, the idea that such a state as Ohio is part of the Mid*west* is almost inconceivable; everything on the other side of Wyoming is considered "back East." The textile mills of New England have moved en masse to the South. Air conditioning has given birth to booming Houston. And so on and on. Much of regional reality is fixed: climate, rainfall, natural resources, capital infrastructure (although even these are subject to human influence). But much of that reality is defined by characteristics that change over time and according to one's preferences. As Hans Landsberg demonstrates in chapter 3, regional politics can make for some strange bedfellows. Regions are geography, but they also can be much more.

Regional Conflict

Disputes between regions are as American as apple pie. Conflicts up to and including the armed variety occurred well before the Civil War, for example, and indeed were a primary cause for abandoning the Articles of Confederation. The Civil War and Reconstruction marked the nation indelibly, and, in the century or so that followed, scores of lesser conflicts provide historical benchmarks.

Several current conflicts—and all those on which we focus in this book—involve natural resources. Thus, energy-poor regions grapple with those that nature has graced with oil, natural gas, or coal. Arid regions struggle for scarce water supplies. Environmentally clean areas resist the exportation of air- and waterborne pollutants from heavily industrialized areas. None of this is surprising: land and its attributes and services may be the oldest sources of social contention. And it is all but guaranteed by the sheer size and diversity of the United States. In a 1942 trip around the country as a "war correspondent," Alistair Cooke learned "that in a continent of (then) forty-eight governments, a half-dozen radically different climates, a score of separate economies, and a goulash of ethnic ingredients, nothing that you could say about the whole country is going to be true."[2] As the Smithsonian Institution put it in a Bicentennial exhibit, this truly is "a nation of nations." The absence of conflict in such a stew would be surprising.

What is new is the sudden and pervasive importance of energy as a generator of regional fractiousness. The oil price shocks of the 1970s in effect redefined wealth, and the production, consumption, and waste products of energy now are key factors in nearly every major current economic, environmental, and social issue. As Christopher K. Leman has phrased it, "Regional issues in energy development present ethical, constitutional, and economic questions that go far beyond simple concepts like greed and envy."[3]

Also new—or at least revived—is the depth of feeling that regional differences now generate. Pithy, not to say nasty, bumperstickers shout out the hostility of Texans for New Englanders, who in turn vilify Montanans for taxing coal. The Southwest envies the Northwest's abundant water, and the Northeast and Midwest—the so-called Snowbelt—believe their industrial lifeblood is draining away toward a rapacious Sunbelt.[4] Feelings are running high, so much so that even Canadian leaders—certainly no strangers to regional conflict—express their shock at the extent and tone of conflcts among U.S. regional representatives.[5]

Resources for the Future mounted a major forum in the fall of 1981 to examine the current spate of regional conflicts in the United States, to place them in perspective, and to assess their implications for national policy. The six papers commissioned for the forum have been revised and edited and form the bulk of this volume. In the next few pages I will present brief summaries of the authors' principal themes and offer an overview of the issues they present.

History and Perspective

In chapter 2, Nathan Rosenberg ranges widely across American history and demonstrates that conflict among regions is a normal state of affairs.

The present round of conflict, he notes, has its source in the development since the Great Depression of a national move "beyond greed and envy" to a position of concern about income distribution. The debate over energy pricing policy, for example, is dominated by questions of fairness or equity. To this notion—grounded solidly on what happens to individuals or groups—Rosenberg adds the perception of *regional* equity. We collectively seem to believe that disparities among regions at the least should not be worsened by national policy, and at best might be ameliorated.

Regional Development

To what degree has economic development produced fair or unfair regional results? In exploring this question, Rosenberg traces agricultural specialization and the advances in mechanization, refrigeration, and transportation that opened the world market to American food and fiber. Of course, agriculture long has been characterized by cycles of boom and bust, a pattern that reinforces the problems of areas that experience losses of labor and capital to regions of greater efficiency. Even given economic fluctuations, however, Rosenberg is impressed by the results of regional specialization coupled with labor and capital mobility—high rates of growth for the nation as a whole and, perhaps surprisingly, converging income differentials among regions. Uneven growth certainly causes pain at some times in some places, but, in the aggregate, all U.S. regions have experienced economic growth and increasing real incomes. Disparities in rates of growth exist, but the direction in all cases—at least since 1880—has been substantially upward.

Indeed, Rosenberg sees the *national* pattern of progress as so striking that he perceives the concern for *regional* equity as both futile and threatening. The danger of defining equity in regional terms, he concludes, is that it may lead to policies to mitigate regional problems at the expense of national efficiency and growth. Over the long haul, he demonstrates, regional economic disparities often are better left alone.

Energy "Haves" and "Have-Nots"

In chapter 3, Hans H. Landsberg views current regional conficts through the prism of the energy "crisis" precipitated by the oil price shocks of the 1970s. In particular, he examines two main components of the popular Snowbelt-versus-Sunbelt notion. Have income and employment shifted from energy-poor to energy-rich areas? And—again the question of equity—how unevenly are the burdens of high energy prices distributed around the country?

With regard to the first question, Landsberg resists the temptation to seize on a few suggestive statistics as proof of a major move of income and employment to the energy-surplus states. It is true that population growth is shifting from the North and East toward the South and West, and that this is consistent with a theory based on energy prices. But it also is true that these shifts are continuations of trends at least four decades old. The energy component—if there is one—is masked by the overall trend. The data for per capita income distribution are similarly suggestive and inconclusive, lost for now at least in the overall trend of converging regional incomes.

Landsberg analyzes in considerable depth the unequal burdens borne by different regions because of differing climates, energy endowments, and fuel uses, among other factors. He documents what every New Englander knows without the benefit of comprehensive statistics: cold winters and heavy reliance on expensive fuel oil make the Northeast the area hardest hit by high energy prices. This does indeed make for regional divisiveness, but Landsberg sees this diminishing as the 1980s progress, largely because of likely price hikes for the natural gas and electricity that now account for lower prices elsewhere in the country. As energy prices become more equal, regionally differential pain will be less acute. Cold winters will remain, of course, but they are at least as cold in Wyoming as in Massachusetts.

Future Problems

For Landsberg, the principal worry for future regional conflict lies in the application of severance taxes—taxes on minerals (or forest products) assessed when they are removed from the soil—by states amply endowed with fuel minerals. The most celebrated current example is Montana's tax on coal, but more than twenty other states also assess severance taxes. Energy-deficient regions can and do become highly exercised over this concept, despite its present marginal impact on consumer prices, and the friction it generates could become intense. Landsberg warns, however, that seeking to mitigate the effects of severance taxes or any other regionally perceived slight due to energy prices could backfire. Shifts in economic activity, including those in population, employment, and investment, he concludes, are appropriate responses to changing prices and availability of energy resources. Government cannot change reality.

Typical Cases Involving Natural Resources

As suggested at the outset, much of the regional conflict now perceived to be at an abnormally high level occurs either in the West itself or has a western component. It therefore is not surprising that the three contemporary cases chosen for review by Allen V. Kneese in chapter 4 are drawn from the Rocky Mountain region (although each also involves other parts of the country). All three involve not only conflicts between and among states, but also between states and the federal government.

Colorado Salinity

Kneese first takes up the case of the Colorado River, which becomes increasingly salt-laden as it flows toward Mexico. Salt springs, salt leached from earth and rock, and salt in return-flow irrigation water all contribute to the load, but major recent additions to the Colorado's salinity can be chalked up to upstream states, which divert much of the water, preventing it from diluting the downstream concentration of salts. The upstream states thus impose what economists call external costs—in this case, the costs of saline pollution—on downstream states, and both impose them on Mexico, which is left with a salty trickle. The "solution" is an international treaty that permits both the upstream and downstream states to resolve their differences by shifting the costs involved to the United States as a whole, that is, to all U.S. taxpayers. Kneese weighs all the interests involved, asks why the United States is willing to strike an economically bad bargain *vis-à-vis* Mexico, and predicts the salinity issue will rise again.

The Montana Coal Tax

Expanding on the severance tax question raised by Landsberg, Kneese focuses on Montana's controversial tax on coal. The controversy is generated not only by the high level of the tax—30 percent of the coal's value—but also because most of the coal subject to it is mined on federal land and used out of state. The result has been a succession of court battles instigated by certain Montana coal producers and out-of-state utility companies. In July 1981, the U.S. Supreme Court decided in favor of the state.

Kneese chronicles in detail the legal precedents and issues involved in the Supreme Court's decision and looks at congressional attempts (introduced both before and after the decision) to set limits to taxes and fees on mineral extraction. The stakes are high, in both dollar and political terms. On the one hand, the Court's ruling permits states to set rates however high they wish. But on the other, Congress may be on the way to regulating state and local taxes on everything that enters interstate commerce.

Nuclear Wastes

In May 1981, the state of New Mexico filed a complaint in U.S. District Court against the U.S. Department of Energy, charging that the state's rights had been violated in DOE's attempt to establish a nuclear waste repository—the Waste Isolation Pilot Plant—in New Mexico. In his final case study, Kneese examines the WIPP controversy and assesses the state's contention, among other claims, that its Tenth Amendment constitutional rights were violated by the federal government. This approach is especially interesting in light of a Supreme Court presumably more sympathetic to states' rights claims than its predecessors. More broadly, Kneese's analysis raises the questions of what are the costs and benefits to a state asked to perform a service in the nation's interest, and how they should be allocated.

Legal Structure of Interstate Resource Conflicts

Richard B. Stewart argues in chapter 5 that traditional governmental mechanisms of accommodation and resolution have been overstressed by some of the conflicts generated by high energy prices, by resulting pressures to develop the West, and by environmental insults, including increased public sensitivity to them as well as their specific impacts. The adequacy of our institutions to deal with such conflicts clearly must be reexamined, he believes, and he launches such a review with an examination of their legal bases in the Articles of Confederation, the Constitution, and succeeding interpretations by the U.S. Supreme Court, including four rulings handed down by the Court during its 1980 term.

Judicial Deference

In the past, the federal courts have taken the initiative in deciding conflicts between states and in invalidating state regulation and taxation that restrict the free flow of capital and labor through the national economy. But in the four recent cases—including the Montana severance tax case—the Supreme Court made clear that the federal judiciary will not play a major role in resolving conflicts among states over natural resources. Stewart agrees that in some cases this judicial deference is desirable. But in an important class of cases—those involving out-of-state impacts that are not economic—he finds the Court's reluctance unwarranted. Transboundary pollution, such as acid rain, is a prime example. Bargaining among states rarely can resolve such conflicts, he says, and Congress encounters substantial constitutional and political obstacles barring the way to legislative solutions.

Stewart is not surprised that the judicial techniques developed to maintain an open-market economy have been found wanting in environmental and natural resource controversies, where nonmarket values often are uppermost. New approaches are needed, he urges, and he offers a few for consideration.

Externality, Conflict, and Decision

In chapter 6, Clifford S. Russell establishes a three-part categorization of resource and environmental conflicts based on the concept of external costs or externalities—pecuniary, real, and political externalities.

Pecuniary Externalities

Market interactions, such as when a new source of supply drives down the price an existing firm can charge for its product, can result in costs to that firm not of its own making. Is society responsible for mitigating these costs when they may result in, say, the failure of a major company or industry, or when they are caused by state taxes on energy resources? Not often, Russell suggests. Such effects are the signals that drive the national economy, and to the extent society tries to switch a signal by blocking a pecuniary externality it distorts adjustments to changes in reality.

Real Externalities

When an emitter pollutes a water source or airshed used by others, it imposes a real externality on them. These are more difficult to deal with than the pecuniary variety, especially when they take the form of state policies that create or permit real spillovers into other states. Real externalities often require social management, Russell argues, but he finds the common devices for so doing—for example, regional institutions, and recourse to the courts—not quite up to the task.

Political Externalities

The design of political institutions, jurisdictions, and decision processes results in situations in which out-of-state citizens are prevented from participating in decisions in which they have a legitimate interest. For example, a state may close its borders to radioactive waste disposal and thereby shift the costs of handling such wastes to other states. Russell finds the mechanisms for dealing with such political externalities even weaker and more *ad hoc* than those for real externalities, and he calls for the creation of more imaginative institutions to do so. For example, he raises the possibility of "contracting into" a nongeographic jurisdiction by agreeing in advance to share whatever costs are involved if one's view prevailed.

Above all, Russell emphasizes the futility of making long-run policy to protect short-run interests. The preservation of the ability to adapt to changing conditions, he concludes, should be the key to national policy.

Epilogue

The RFF Forum on Regional Conflict and National Policy was capped by Gilbert F. White's summary and assessment of the day's presentations. His Epilogue to this volume provides the same service—a drawing together of separate strands, a certain perspective, a sense of closure.

White sees three new factors that distinguish present regional conflicts from those that have characterized the United States since before its beginnings. The first is the radically changed energy situation that has created both immense new values on those lands endowed with energy mineral resources and new inequities among regions.

Second—and related to the real and perceived disparities generated by higher-valued energy—is the rising concern for equity, not only as it concerns income among regions, but also in terms of fairness to future generations.

Third, White cites the maturation of environmental values to the point where the environmental impact of technological changes is a legitimate, even routine, target of public appraisal. Energy, equity, and environment have changed the framework of regional debate, he asserts, and have increased the importance of resource analysis in informing that debate.

Although a different cast of characters might well have produced a different volume, White concludes from the evidence presented that the prognosis for the future is essentially benign. Given time and prudent selection of policy measures, regional conflicts need not become deeply divisive or disruptive.

Finally, White suggests an intriguing scenario of the future. Might not a concern for global atmospheric problems, say, or for world food supplies lead to a world view that subordinates regional to national interests?

Conclusions

The sometimes hyperbolic tone of the news media when discussing regional problems may suggest something both new and darkly portentous. Yet as touched on above and developed in full later, regional conflict is older than the Republic. Indeed, who would think it extraordinary? No one considers it strange that, say, Norwegians and Spaniards have different cultures, customs, economies, politics, and other distinguishing characteristics, yet Norway and Spain are no more geographically separate than are Maine and Florida; all of Europe could be tucked between Georgia and Oregon. The continental scope and cultural breadth of its peoples assures the United States of conflict along with diversity, and both can be healthy as well as divisive.

One even can wonder at the relatively low level of disagreement in the United States. Compare the minor frictions of the Snowbelt-versus-Sunbelt confrontation, for example, with the disputes plaguing Belgium, Spain, Canada, Iran, Nigeria, or other countries where regional differences loom large. U.S. regional conflict is important, but it is not nation threatening.

Westering

Why does so much of the conflict that does occur seem to happen in the West? Among other factors—water obviously is critical, for example—two stand out because of their dynamism, their importance, and their relationship to each other.

First, as documented in chapter 3, the population of the country has not only grown enormously in two-plus centuries, but also it has shifted decidedly westward. During the 1970s, the region with the nation's oldest urban settlements—the Northeast—actually recorded an absolute decline in population. Washington, D.C., was close to the population center of the country when it became the nation's capital in 1800, but that center now has marched across the Mississippi. I will leave to the readers of political tea leaves to estimate how much the westward flow of population has contributed to the propensity of politicians to "run against Washington," even while living and working in the capital, but surely the shift west has changed both political and economic realities and perceptions. In the context of regional conflicts concerning natural resources and the environment, the influx of people to regions previously sparsely populated could not fail to generate friction over land and water and their products and services.

The related factor is the sudden emergence of energy commodities as critical; it is no coincidence that the single most discussed case in this book is that of Montana's severance tax on coal. To an important degree, U.S. energy resources—oil, natural gas, oil shale, coal, uranium, geothermal, even solar—are western energy resources and, despite the westward tilt of population, the West still is relatively underpopulated; in Leman's apt shorthand, "Energy is where people aren't."[6]

Thus, two tides merge and conflict. The West is getting both more people and more energy development, and the results are boomtowns, water scarcity, air pollution, severance tax disputes, swiftly changing economies and life-styles, Sagebrush Rebellions—in short, the whole range of simmering issues that prompted this volume.

Culture

Since it is impossible for one set of authors to cover every possible nuance of regional change and conflict, it is only fair to warn the reader about what is not in the book. The most important omission, I think, is what might be called the people factor. There is little in the way of demographics, for example, and nothing about religion, values, ethnicity, or motivation. Yet obviously peoples' hopes and fears matter a great deal.

Nationalism may be the most potent force working on today's world, and U.S. regions are not immune to such emotional ties. One can only speculate—to take one of the most clear-cut examples—about the regional and national influence of the country's Spanish-speaking population in general and of Americans of Mexican descent in particular. Already the largest city in the largest state is second only to Mexico City in its population of Mexicans. And Los Angeles in many ways is a bellwether for the rest of the country. This is not to suggest any specific pictures of the future, but rather to underline that what is not covered in the pages to follow may be at least as important as what is. There are subjects enough for several other books.

Lessons

A private planner or a public policymaker cannot glean from this book a list of do's and don'ts for proper regional management. Were the topic so easily handled it would not have been necessary to deal with it in such depth.

Nevertheless, the authors separately and concurrently do offer guidelines that could usefully be observed, especially at the national level. In outline they might read as follows.

Take the long view, for over a period of years what appears to be regional disaster may, in fact, pave the way for long-term growth and progress. Or conversely, as Russell puts it, do not make long-run policy to protect short-run interests.

Focus on people, not regions, because economic growth and change necessarily involve substantial shifts in the regional distribution of economic activity. Regional welfare matters, but not at the expense of national welfare.

Pay attention to prices and availabilities of natural resources, the signals that move the gears and levers of a well-functioning market economy. Energy prices are a case in point: the nation would have been much better off had price controls not been in effect when oil prices jumped fourfold in 1974.

Do not struggle against the tide, for many negative things are going to happen regardless of what government tries to do about them. Can government prevent the decline of a regionally based industry that no longer is competitive? Even if it could, should it, since it could be done only at a cost to the rest of the nation? The federal government certainly should attempt the practical when dealing with regional ills, but it should shun the impractical as both costly and futile.

Above all, be open to change. The central message of the book is that change, flexibility, adaptation, and growth have been essential—perhaps even definitive—characteristics of the American experience. As White says, growth and change are as natural for a nation as for a cell or organism. What has marked America is its ability to respond positively to change by maintaining flexible political, economic, and legal institutions.

Those who have followed RFF research and publications over the years are aware that this excursion into regional problems has been preceded by a great deal of scholarly work. A 1960 book, *Regions, Resources, and Economic Growth,* contains a passage that presages the chapters to follow so well that it bears quotation in full.

> . . . Though there are still differential advantages for production and consumption to be had within the national framework, the progressive equalization of per capita income among the regions at higher levels, not excluding the Southeast, is proof that the national economy as a whole is potentially greater than any of its parts, provided the parts are differentiated along lines of comparative advantage. All regions have eventually come to share in the larger abundance.
>
> If the play of technology on resources has been a primary factor in the growth and redistribution of the nation's wealth, a necessary condition has been the opportunity for labor and capital to flow freely throughout the commonwealth, seeking their most profitable employ-

ment in resource development, manufacture, or servicing, as the case may be. In the course of this general amelioration some regions, New England for example, have made painful adjustments; wide areas of the country have been ruthlessly and in some cases, perhaps, needlessly denuded of their natural endowment. Coal mines have been exhausted, rich ores depleted, forests cut down, and the soil impoverished. Yet, on balance, the American economy, if sometimes terribly wasteful, is not simply a predatory system. In one sense, resources unused are no better than resources abused. Public and private interests have become aware that, having used up the riches of one area, they can no longer expect to return that area to nature and move on to "new frontiers" elsewhere. The frontiers of tomorrow must be found in their own backyard.[7]

The metaphor needs no changing after twenty-two years. The nation's backyards may seem closer together now than at the dawn of the New Frontier, but there still is a premium on neighborliness.

Notes

1. Indeed, Joel Garreau argues that the structure of separate states is all but obsolete and that regional realities are so strong that the United States (and portions of Canada, Mexico, and the Caribbean) constitute a series of clearly identifiable "nations." For a readable and instructive survey of this thesis, see Joel Garreau, *The Nine Nations of North America* (Boston, Mass., Houghton Mifflin, 1981).

2. Alistair Cooke, *America* (New York, Alfred A. Knopf, 1973) p. 13.

3. Christopher K. Leman, ed., *Regional Issues in Energy Development: A Dialogue of East and West,* Harvard Center for International Affairs Policy Paper No. 2 (Cambridge, Mass., University Consortium for Research on North America, September 1981) p. 9.

4. For example, here is the anguished perception of Rep. Robert W. Edgar (D–Pa.), chairman of the Northeast–Midwest Congressional Coalition, speaking before the House Budget Committee, on March 22, 1982:

> It is my clear belief that there is an inherent and unmistakable bias in the Administration's budget proposals against the older states that our coalition represents. The already hard-pressed states of the Northeast and Midwest are being asked to bear the greatest burden at a time when their economies can least afford it. We realize that all Americans and all states must make sacrifices if we are to restore our national economic health. However, the biases that are so apparent in the President's proposal run the risk of inflicting further long-term damage on the economy of our region, damage that ultimately would subvert achievement of the President's objectives.
>
> In an overall sense, we are concerned that the President's budget focuses solely on broad-brushed economic trends, and fails to recognize the fact that ours no longer is a nation—and perhaps never was—where national unemployment rates, national inflation rates, and Gross National Product tell the whole economic story. The national economy has devolved into several separate and distinct regional economies, each with its own strengths and weaknesses and its own claim on Federal resources. America is no longer a nation where all boats rise and fall on the same tide. Levels of economic growth and levels of investment mean something quite different in our inner cities than in some of our more affluent and growing communities ["Washington Talk" page, *The New York Times*, April 20, 1982].

5. Leman, *Regional Issues,* pp. 3–4.

6. Ibid., p. 12.

7. Harvey S. Perloff, Edgar S. Dunn, Jr., Eric E. Lampard, and Richard F. Muth, *Regions, Resources, and Economic Growth* (Baltimore, Md., Johns Hopkins University Press for Resources for the Future, 1960) p. 291.

chapter two

History and Perspective

Nathan Rosenberg

One of the legacies of the 1970s is a heightened awareness of apparent conflicts among different regions of the country. The immediate cause appears to be concern about energy in the aftermath of the 1973–74 Arab oil embargo, intensified by the realization that some regions were much better off than others in responding to the problems of the so-called energy crisis.

Fuel was added to the fire of apparent regional conflict by new locutions in the news media as reporters and pundits attempted to dramatize the uneven regional incidence of the "crisis." Thus, controversies between energy-exporting and energy-importing regions were characterized as conflicts between "Sunbelt" and "Snowbelt." The public became aware of something darkly referred to as the "Sagebrush Rebellion." Spokespersons for energy-rich states spoke with increasing resentment of Yankee exploitation. The doctrine of states' rights appeared suddenly to be accorded a new lease on life. Almost inevitably, the specter of an "energy civil war" rose into public view.

History offers some useful perspectives on present concerns. Indeed, many aspects of interregional resource conflicts repeat themes as old as our federal system of government. That is, however, hardly a point that needs belaboring in a country whose most traumatic historical experience was a bloody fratricidal war. Certainly not all regional disputes carry the seed of potential civil war, but history can be scanned for an appreciation of the implications of different courses of action in dealing with regional conflicts of several lesser sorts.

The Frontier Thesis

To an extent that is more true of America than most countries, our history can be understood only as a composite of the history of separate regions. The sheer continental magnitude of the country has made this inevitable. But, moreover, a large part of U.S. history *is* the history of the progressive geographic expansion of people into diverse climatic, topographic, and natural resource environments. It is surely no accident that the most influential single force in American historiography has been Frederick Jackson Turner's hypothesis that one should look to the unique aspects of life on the frontier for a deeper understanding of the forces shaping American institutions and character.[1] Turner's frontier thesis, first essayed in 1893, has shaped the research interests and strategies of several generations of American historians. While some monograph writers have concentrated on the distinctive features of different frontiers—the Great Plains, the Rocky Mountains, the Pacific Northwest, and so on—the political historians have focused on the series of compromises involved in perpetuating a federal system comprising divergent and often centrifugal regional interest groups.

States, Regions, Controversy

The westward movement was critically important to the federal structure because the organization of territories into states constantly threatened to upset the balance of power within that structure. From the Missouri Compromise of 1820 through the Compromise of 1850, the Kansas–Nebraska Act of 1854, and the final cataclysm following southern secession in 1861, the central political issue was regional domination of the federal government. And this question incessantly was thrust into the center of American political life by the westward movement of the frontier. "Even the slavery struggle," Turner argued, ". . . occupies its important place in American history because of its relation to westward expansion."[2]

Even on issues that did not appear to be—and indeed were not—explicitly regional in substance, well-defined regional positions usually developed that reflected the interests of the dominant groups of each region. The essential reason then, as now, is that these positions were based on calculations of regional and local incidence of costs and benefits. If, for simplicity, we consider the three major, well-defined antebellum regions—a manufacturing North, an agricultural West, and a cotton-producing South—we could show that, on the four great economic issues of the tariff, internal improvements, alienation of public lands, and banking and credit policy, calculations of anticipated regional incidence dominated the pattern of congressional voting behavior. Indeed, it would be surprising only if this were not so. It is useful to recall, for example, that the southern states raised the doctrine of nullification (the view that states could reject and fail to enforce federal legislation of which they disapproved) long before the Civil War, and in a context quite independent of the issue of slavery. When it was raised—or, more accurately, revived—it was in the context of implacable southern opposition to the high tariff levels established by Congress in 1824 and 1828. The South raised the doctrine of nullification because it accurately perceived high tariffs as a serious threat to its economic interests. High tariffs arguably might benefit a North anxious to encourage a nascent industrialism. To a South increasingly linked to European markets for its staple cotton exports and as a source of low-priced industrial imports, high tariffs were an "abomination," as southern spokesmen characterized them at the time.

Changing Times

Although regional economic conflict is a large and integral part of our national history, the framework of that conflict has changed considerably in the past fifty years or so. For example, the establishment of a federal income tax was a decisive triumph of centralizing forces over regional and local forces. In contests over the geographic distribution of federal funds (an ever-larger share of the Gross National Product), the income tax has added an entirely new dimension to regional conflict.

Moreover, since the rise of the modern welfare state out of the ashes of the Great Depression and the collective effort of World War II, new issues or policy alternatives increasingly have been judged in terms of their impact on the distribution of income. American society, as a whole, has become much more concerned with equity considerations than it was in the nineteenth century. Although the egalitarian ethic often is vague and difficult to define precisely in terms of its application or even relevance in specific contexts, it is nonetheless a real and powerful force. The recent debates over energy policy—especially pricing policy—and Social Security, for example, are dominated by considerations of fairness.

Nor are equity considerations confined to issues affecting individuals. More and more now equity is weighed not only in terms of individuals, but also in terms of something called regions—loose geographic units larger than a state and smaller than the nation and presumably with some objective characteristic of homogeneity. But how are regions defined? One can identify those regions that have played important roles in our national history, but establishing unambiguous objective criteria for regions is another matter. Different criteria lead to the identification of very different geographic entities, and most criteria are confronted with continua of variation, with no well-defined, or discrete, boundaries. For example, the widespread notion that the Sunbelt is an energy-exporting region and the Snowbelt an energy-importing region does not fit the facts that Florida, certainly a Sunbelt state, is a heavy energy importer, and that Wyoming, in the middle of the Snowbelt, is a heavy energy exporter.

Nevertheless, in spite of all the ambiguities inherent in defining regions, we are confronted with a range of problems having at their core some notion of regional equity. We therefore must address regional history as a central question. How different are regional economic growth experiences? Is there evidence of regional convergence or divergence, particularly with respect to income distribution? What economic forces underlie these trends? What is the probable impact, on regions and on national growth performance, of a range of possible policy directions that are receiving prominent attention?

Environmental Equity

In recent years concerns about the influence of national policies on regional income and employment have been joined by a growing awareness of the ways in which economic activities generate a variety of undesirable side effects. Perhaps "awareness" is not the right term. People were aware fifty or one hundred years ago of many of these consequences, but either they appeared to be unalterable facts of industrial life or it was implicitly taken for granted that the dollar or disruption costs to deal with them were so high as not to warrant serious consideration.

Now the more or less passive acceptance of pollution, safety, and health hazards has been replaced by a much greater sensitivity to such intrusions and by a determination to reduce their impacts. Thus, at the federal level, many agencies, laws, and regulations aimed at some sort of environmental improvement have become an integral part of our national life. The Clean Air and Clean Water Acts, the Toxic Substances Control Act, the Environmental Protection Agency, the Occupational Safety and Health Administration, and other examples of the new commitment might have their sails trimmed to prevailing political breezes, but they are not likely to be abandoned in the face of what appears to be strong national consensus.

Environmentalism and the Quality of Life

It is useful to consider these federal initiatives in a longer-term perspective. A common undergraduate reaction is that they were made necessary by the unprecedented extent to which a predatory industrial capitalism systematically throws up dangers to health and safety. To take only one of several examples, many of them regard it as axiomatic that it was the automobile that first polluted an otherwise pristine urban environment. When the question is raised whether New York or London is obviously more polluted or less healthy or less safe today than in 1850 or 1900, many students find it difficult to believe that the question is intended seriously. When confronted with the information that New York City contained 150,000 horses in 1900, and that that must have created some pollution and health hazards, it is obvious that most students never have given the matter serious thought.

My purpose here is not just to establish that young people, even at elite universities, are ignorant of even the recent social and economic history of their country, although that is both true and depressing. The more relevant point is that we systematically are raising the standards by which we judge the performance of our social system in many of its basic aspects. Surely it is eminently desirable that we should do so. Indeed, one could argue that a great deal of our progress as a society may be gauged precisely by the evidence of these rising standards. At the same time, it is important that policies be developed with as full recognition as possible of the nature of the tradeoffs between material progress, on the one hand, and environmental protection, broadly defined, on the other.

The distinction often is drawn between further improvements in the material standard of living and improvements in what is called "quality of life." But it is far from clear, even in a society as affluent as that of the United States, whether most people would accept that improvements in the quality of their lives could be divorced from increases in their purchasing power over goods and services. Obviously, purchasing power determines the kinds of houses people live in, the quality and variety of food they eat, the opportunity to spend their leisure time in satisfying ways, the nature of the educational opportunities available to their children and, to some degree at least, their health and life expectancy. Thus, it is easy to pose too sharply the need to choose *either* more material goods *or* improved quality of life. Insofar as such statements merely emphasize that there are different possible social priorities, they are reasonable enough. But the either–or choice is misleading to the extent it neglects the truth that, for many people, improvements in *their* quality of life, as *they* define quality, can come only with an expanding flow of goods and services.

Regional Specialization

In order to appreciate some of the problems posed by a growing preoccupation with "regional equity," defined broadly to include these environmental considerations, we must look at the historical relations between regional development and national development.

Most of the historical studies of long-term economic growth and industrialization have been carried out at a national level of aggregation. For many purposes and for many reasons—not the least being the sources of the data—the nation is regarded as the basic unit of account. In reality, of course, these national accounts are really a composite of smaller units, going all the way down to individuals and households. For present purposes, however, our interest is at the level of the region, and this is highly appropriate: a changing pattern of regional specialization always has been at the center of the process of economic growth and its material benefits.

At any given moment the regional distribution of economic activity reflects geographic differences in resource endowments, access to transportation facilities linking local industry to more distant markets, and market conditions shaping the demand for the products of a particular region, as well as the chain of substitutes for its distinctive resources. In some cases, location is rather rigidly dictated by certain facts of geology, whether it is lead in Missouri, copper in Michigan, or iron ore in western Pennsylvania. Similarly, the location of running water, to be exploited either by water wheel or by a turbine generating electric power, also is dictated by nature, with important consequences for energy-intensive industries. More subtly, agricultural specialization produced by a combination of such conditions as rainfall, topography, soil chemistry, and temperature variation, has led to well-defined patterns of regional specialization, so that it eventually became possible to identify Cotton Belts, Wheat Belts, Corn Belts, Tobacco Belts, and so on. In some cases, peculiar conditions of suitability may lead to extreme dependence on a single location. For example, although California produces about one-half of all U.S. fruits and vegetables, 90 percent of all artichokes produced in America are grown within a few miles of Castroville, California.

The Transportation Factor

These and other patterns of regional specialization have been highly sensitive to transportation costs. In a world of high transportation costs, population is relatively dispersed in rural locations, and industrial activity necessarily is in small units catering to limited, local markets. Even when technical change brings about substantial opportunities for low-cost production through economies of scale, these techniques will not become economical until transportation costs are low enough to permit the movement of goods over a wide geographic region. In this sense, regional specialization, urbanization, and transportation innovation all are closely linked.

The combination of large and growing urban populations and falling transportation costs made possible a high degree of regional specialization in agriculture. In the United States this may be said to have begun with the opening, in 1825, of the Erie Canal, a facility that provided a cheap, all-water route to the eastern seaboard for the products of midwestern agriculture. The opening of the canal also marked the beginning of the decline of older patterns of regional specialization, such as the protracted decline of New England agriculture. (A sad, but apposite footnote to that decline was the 1981 passage of a "right-to-farm" bill in New Hampshire. As reported in the press, the bill was essential to the farmers in the southern counties of the state who were confronting a high risk of lawsuits from nonfarm residents who were indignant over the smell of manure.[3])

To a considerable extent, the story of productivity growth in American agriculture in the nineteenth century has been composed of mechanization plus changing patterns of regional specialization.[4] The two phenomena were in fact highly interdependent. The productivity-increasing effects of the mechanization of cereal crops were vastly greater in the Midwest than they would have been in the rocky, uneven terrain of the Northeast. In the South, Eli Whitney's cotton gin, introduced in 1793, had major locational consequences in addition to its labor-saving impact. The cotton gin, by sharply reducing the cost of seed removal, made it economically feasible to raise short-staple upland cotton, thus extending cotton culture far beyond its earlier confinement to coastal regions. Similarly, the later mechanization of cotton cultivation shifted the comparative advantage for this crop away from the hilly terrain and small farms of the old Southeast to the broad flatlands of the Southwest, where the machinery could be exploited much more efficiently.

With the expansion of the railroad network and refrigeration in the second half of the nineteenth century, the meat supply of an entire country could be heavily concentrated in a single region, while other regions could concentrate on, say, grain products, or fruits and vegetables. Eventually this spreading pattern of specialization became international. During the same period, the large iron steamship with a much-improved marine steam engine made it possible for European consumers to enjoy food products drawn from the continental interiors of North and South America and even Australia. Many of these same Europeans, when they went to work in their textile mills, found themselves working with American cotton and Australian wool.

The adjustments dictated by these changing patterns of world specialization sometimes were sudden and severe, as in the case of British farming. As the cost of transporting a bushel of wheat from Chicago to

Liverpool in 1902 dropped to less than a quarter of what it had been in the 1870s, the competition from the American heartland (and elsewhere) forced a decline in the total English acreage in wheat of more than one-half between 1870 and 1910.

The high degree of agricultural specialization, linked by low transportation costs to world markets, brought instability as well as growth. In the closing decades of the last century, farm incomes fluctuated widely. The variability of climate and rainfall in some remote part of the world might lead to large swings in supply and therefore price. Australia, Argentina, South Africa, and the Ukraine all were substantial contributors to the world wheat market in the late nineteenth century (as was even India for a time). On the other hand, periods of high prices were likely to lead to intermittent surges of overexpansion into locations that could support a prosperous agriculture only when prices were high or climatic conditions unusually favorable. But the very process of rapid expansion often would bring lower prices and incomes in its wake, even at highly productive agricultural locations.

Regional Convergence

The adjustment process in agriculture is highly pertinent to broader questions of regional growth and equity. The point is that, in a society with a high degree of mobility and strong economic motivation, substantial regional differentials in wages or profits can be expected to lead to the movement of labor and capital into those regions (and industries) where the prospective returns are higher. Of course, this equilibrating mechanism never has worked perfectly. Indeed, in view of the fact that decisions to move resources from one location to another always must be made in the shadow of many uncertainties concerning the future, it is not even entirely clear what "perfectly" would mean in this context. In any case, agriculture displayed considerable asymmetry. Farmers did not reduce production during periods of falling prices as readily as they expanded it during periods of rising prices, an asymmetry that underlay a good deal of federal agricultural policy in the twentieth century. Nevertheless, taking the scale of the country into account, one must be impressed by the high degree of factor mobility in the nineteenth century. These regional movements have been indispensible contributors to high aggregate rates of growth for the entire economy.

These movements have had another consequence of critical historical importance. Quite simply, each such movement has served to narrow the income differential that gave rise to the movement in the first place. Impressive evidence exists of a long-term trend—at least since 1880—toward the narrowing of income differentials among regions.[5]

Economic historians have pushed quantitative estimates of personal income differentials by region as far back as 1840, when the average income of the Northeast was about a third higher than the national average (see table 2–1).[6] In the agricultural South and West,[7] personal incomes averaged between two-thirds and three-quarters of the national average, with the striking exception of the so-called West South Central area, where the flourishing commerce and sugarcane agriculture of Louisiana gave that division the highest per capita income in the country. The figures for the South as a whole, of course, incorporate the legal and institutional peculiarities of slavery. The income level of the southern white population in 1840 was above the national average.

No drastic changes occurred between 1840 and 1860 in relative per capita income levels by region, and certainly no strong evidence exists of a narrowing of regional differentials. The period between 1860 and 1880 is dominated by the devastating impact of the Civil War and its aftermath, especially the destruction and disruption visited upon southern agriculture. For the South as a whole, per capita income as a per-

Table 2–1. Personal Income Per Capita in Each Region as Percentage of U.S. Average, Selected Years 1840–1950

Regions	1840	1860	1880	1900	1920	1930	1940	1950
Total United States	100	100	100	100	100	100	100	100
Total Northeast	135	139	141	137	132	138	124	115
New England	132	143	141	134	124	129	121	109
Middle Atlantic	136	137	141	139	134	140	124	116
Total North Central	68	68	98	103	100	101	103	106
East North Central	67	69	102	106	108	111	112	112
West North Central	75	66	90	97	87	82	84	94
Total South	76	72	51	51	62	55	65	72
South Atlantic	70	65	45	45	59	56	69	74
East South Central	73	68	51	49	52	48	55	62
West South Central	144	115	60	61	72	61	70	80
Total West	—	—	190	163	122	115	125	114
Mountain	—	—	168	139	100	83	92	96
Pacific	—	—	204	163	135	130	138	121

Source: Richard A. Easterlin, "Regional Income Trends, 1840–1950," in Seymour Harris, ed., *American Economic History* (New York, McGraw-Hill, 1961) p. 528. Used with permission of McGraw-Hill Book Company.

centage of the U.S. average fell from 72 percent in 1860 to 51 percent in 1880. But after 1880 a distinct long-term trend emerges and dominates the regional income data right through the twentieth century—a conspicuous narrowing of per capita regional income differences. This narrowing does not occur either smoothly or uniformly—it was much more significant and pervasive between 1930 and 1950 than in the three previous decades—but it appears indisputable that, within the high aggregative growth performance of the American economy after 1880, powerful adjustment mechanisms were working toward a convergence of regional incomes. The regional movement of capital and labor, and changes in the structure of employment within regions, were the principal agents of changes. Thus, whereas in 1900 the region with the highest per capita income (the far West) had a per capita income 3.4 times as great as the region with the lowest per capita income (the Southeast), by 1977 that figure had shrunk to a far more modest level of 1.3 (see table 2–2).[8]

As the demographic aspects of these long-term regional trends are not of primary interest to this volume, suffice it to say that a major aspect of narrowing differences indeed has been population movements. The lure of a variety of newly opened mining frontiers in the nineteenth century, the migration to California in the 1930s and after World War II, the prolonged movement of the rural black population of the South to northern cities (and to southern cities), and the long-term structural shift of the labor force out of agriculture and into industrial and service employment obviously have played major roles.

An additional aspect of the post-1880 narrowing of regional income differentials is extremely important. Namely, while relative income lev-

Table 2–2. Regional Per Capita Income as Percentage of U.S. Average, Selected Years, 1900–77

Region	1900	1930	1950	1960	1970	1975	1977
New England	133.7	129.2	107	110	100	103	102
Mideast	137.7	142.6	117	116	113	109	107
Great Lakes	106.2	109.6	111	108	104	104	106
Plains	97.0	61.7	95	93	95	98	94
Southeast	47.8	50.2	68	73	82	86	86
Southwest	68.4	64.3	87	87	89	93	94
Rocky Mountain	145.2	86.2	97	94	91	94	95
Far West	162.9	130.8	120	116	111	111	111

Source: Advisory Commission on Intergovernmental Relations, *Regional Growth: Historic Perspective* (Washington, D.C., June 1980) p. 11.

els indeed have changed a great deal, it would be wrong to conclude that some regional divisions have gained at the expense of absolute declines in others. In fact, with the exception of the post-Civil War period in the South, the process has been remarkably benign. Although great disparities are evident in regional *rates* of growth, the long-term trend in absolute income levels has been substantially upward in each region.

Equity's Threat to Positive Change

The persistent convergence of regional incomes over the past century is all the more remarkable because equilibrating forces quite obviously have been accompanied by such disequilibrating forces as shifts in the composition of demand that alter the remuneration to specific productive agents, and dynamic forces that lie at the heart of productivity improvement and long-term economic growth—resource discovery and technological change. Unlike movements of labor and capital that typically work to narrow regional differences, these dynamic forces function more as a "wild card" with respect to regional income differences. Although they play a critical role in raising the aggregate growth rate of the *entire* economy, their effect on regional differentials is much more difficult to predict.[9]

Discovery and Change

Although resource discovery and technological change often are referred to as if they were two entirely separate forces, that is not always the case. In many instances, technological change serves very much the same economic purposes, and generates many similar results, as does a resource discovery. New drilling techniques that make the extraction of offshore oil possible for the first time expands the total available resource base every bit as much as the discovery of a new inland oil field. New processing technology that makes possible the cheap exploitation of low-grade taconite iron ores is tantamount to the discovery of new high-grade iron ore deposits. Developing a chemical technique such as creosoting that drastically increases the life of railroad ties is functionally similar to discovering an unexploited stand of timber. The development of a new, high-yielding hybrid corn or a process that reduces fertilizer costs compares with the opening up of new tracts of fertile land.

Thus, the relationship of a region's natural resource endowment to its level of economic performance is a good deal more subtle than might appear on first consideration. In a static context resource endowment is a main determinant of regional income levels. But in a more dynamic context, the process of technological change—that may find new uses for old resources as well as techniques for exploiting previously unused resources—continually alters the economic significance of specific resources. Indeed, this process is the essential long-term offset to an otherwise Malthusian world of limited and depletable resources. Technological change serves the essential function of expanding the resource base and thereby providing the material basis for continued economic growth. For example, in a very meaningful sense, having mastered the technology of using low-grade taconite ores in the blast furnace, it is true to say that U.S. deposits of iron ore today are several times as large as they were in 1950.

Regional Equity

It is precisely this process that is being complicated, and perhaps may be jeopardized, by an excessive concern with regional equity. The historical achievements of the American economy were firmly rooted in the great regional diversity of its resource base, combined with a high degree of human and institutional flexibility in adapting to changing patterns of resource needs. It is in the nature of a dynamic technology that it generates long-term economic growth for a large population through a process that distributes costs and benefits in a highly arbitrary, or fortuitous, fashion. It is a matter of real concern that many of the benefits of this process are diffuse and long-term, while many of the costs are locationally specific, highly visible, and immediately apparent. But an increasing concern with equity is leading to policy litmus tests, based on the effects of changing patterns of resource use, that require some balancing of costs and benefits within narrow geographic units and within time periods of increasingly short duration.

It is easy to understand and to sympathize with these kinds of concerns. Mine accidents and black lung disease are not uniformly distributed over the nation's population, but are heavily concentrated in Appalachia. Off-shore oil drilling does not affect Nebraska or South Dakota, but it may pose serious environmental threats to coastal locations in

California, New Jersey, or Massachusetts. Conversely, a large-scale shale oil industry, should the nation choose to develop one, will be heavily concentrated in a small region of Colorado's western slope and will have no adverse effects on coastal regions. Whatever the hazards of uranium mining turn out to be, they will be borne disproportionately by the Navajo Indians in New Mexico, whose land produces 50 percent of all American reactor uranium.

Similarly, the disposal of toxic chemical and radioactive wastes and the dangers potentially embodied in a Love Canal are highly location-specific. Even acid precipitation, though subject to a number of uncertainties associated with meteorological variables, does not pose anything like a uniform threat to all communities across the country.

Meeting the Policy Test

Nevertheless, the future probably will resemble the past in that economic growth will continue to require substantial shifts in the regional distribution of economic activities and a high degree of regional specialization. A major policy question for government surely will be how to develop programs that ameliorate the local adverse effects of resource development without imposing severe penalties on the operation of the national economy. In developing such policies, a hard and skeptical look needs to be taken at priorities and tradeoffs. Specifically, it is far from clear that justifiable concern about income inequalities should translate into a high priority for policies that reduce regional income inequalities. As noted, regional income differentials already are relatively small by almost any standard. Indeed, it is fair to say that some of the recent eruption of concern about inequality results from the perception in certain parts of the country that regional differentials have become too narrow. Regional differentials are a major component of national income inequalities in, say, Brazil, or Italy, or China, but income inequality in America today has very little to do with regional differentials. Income inequality overwhelmingly is a matter of differences that persist *within* each region, and policies directed toward reducing income inequality by further reductions in regional differentials inevitably must be clumsy and ineffective.

Thus, the danger of defining equity in terms of regional dimensions is that it may lead to policies that have very small favorable effects in terms of equity and very substantial negative effects in terms of national efficiency and growth. Here, as elsewhere, the proper targets of government policy ought to be people, and not regions.

Notes

1. As Turner wrote, ". . . American development has exhibited not merely advance along a single line, but a return to primitive conditions on a continually advancing frontier line, and a new development for that area. American social development has been continually beginning over again on the frontier. This perennial rebirth, this fluidity of American life, this expansion westward with its new opportunities, its continuous touch with the simplicity of primitive society, furnish the forces dominating American character. The true point of view in the history of this nation is not the Atlantic coast, it is the Great West." See F. J. Turner, "The Significance of the Frontier in American History," in *The Frontier in American History* (New York, Henry Holt, 1920) pp. 2–3.

2. Ibid., p. 3.

3. *The Economist,* May 9, 1981, p. 60.

4. The dramatic increases in agricultural productivity due to varietal improvements depended heavily upon an expanding knowledge of genetics, and are largely a twentieth-century phenomenon.

5. The convergence of regional per capita income differentials as a possible consequence of changing energy patterns is explored in some detail in chapter 3.

6. See Richard A. Easterlin, "Regional Income Trends, 1840-1950," in Seymour Harris, ed., *American Economic History* (New York, McGraw-Hill, 1961) p. 528.

7. In 1840 the settlement frontier had barely crossed the Mississippi River.

8. Advisory Commission on Intergovernmental Relations, *Regional Growth: Historic Perspective* (Washington, D.C., June 1980) p. 11.

9. One interesting aspect of this "wild card" nature of technological change is that it has included the introduction of certain new industries, for example, electronics, in which natural resource inputs play a relatively minor role. These so-called footloose industries consequently have a considerable degree of freedom in determining their location, and often have chosen sites for their attractive climate or proximity to recreation facilities.

chapter three

Energy "Haves" and "Have-Nots"

Hans H. Landsberg

For many years prior to 1974, when oil export prices were quadrupled by the Organization of Petroleum Exporting Countries (OPEC), energy prices were low in the United States and, in terms of constant dollars, actually were declining. Moreover, after the sudden shock administered by OPEC, prices were relatively stable for five years, again measured in inflation-free dollars. So perhaps it is not surprising that rising energy prices did not cause a great deal of pain in the mid-1970s, nor did they lead to regional bickering. Indeed, one can look back now on the price levels of 1974–79 with nostalgia for the good old days: there was not much to yell or fight about if the issue had been price alone.

But if inflation-corrected prices in hindsight were modest and unexciting, the physical availability of energy—"access," in jargon terms—provoked heated discussion, quick tempers, and occasional fistfights. Gasoline shortages with attending waiting lines were highly concentrated, popping up first on the West Coast, then on the East Coast, and were more prominent in metropolitan than rural areas. Natural gas shortages were equally spotty, causing major difficulties especially in parts of the Midwest. In both instances, the consensus is that the fault lay in the combination of governmental allocation schemes and regulated prices. No North–South or East–West conflict was involved or discussed.

More serious regional implications were associated with aspects of energy production, although it can be argued that the regional dimension was only apparent and that the true conflict was environmental. East Coast resistance to offshore oil drilling, for example, and efforts to block the building of new refineries in Maine and Virginia, were the kinds of episodes that led to the famous Texas bumperstickers reading "Let the bastards freeze in the dark."

Eastern and Western Coal

An environmental issue also plays a significant role in the continuing conflict over sulfur-associated air pollution from coal, a conflict that stems from the provisions of the Clean Air Act of 1970. The act, amended in 1977 and up for reauthorization in 1982, originally mandated certain air quality standards but left the means of achieving them to the polluter. Specifically, it left available to coal-burning utilities the option of using coal with a relatively low sulfur content as one way of reducing sulfur dioxide emissions to the prescribed level.

These provisions increased the attractiveness of western coal. Indeed, coal located west of the Mississippi River, and above all in Wyoming, Montana, and the Dakotas, had several advantages for its user. Its low-sulfur content gave users at least a fighting chance to burn it "au naturel;" it was mined by non-United Mine Workers labor and thus had a better chance of being mined with less labor trouble; it occurred in rich and extensive seams, accessible largely by surface (strip) mining, and producible in supersized mines with modern technology; and finally, the rail transportation system for carrying it east or south was in far better shape than that which served the coal fields east of the Mississippi River.

On the other hand, western coal has a significantly lower heating value, raising mining, transport, and all handling costs per unit of usable heat. And it is far away from most big users, except for parts of the Midwest, although even here the distances are greater than from the nearby coal mines of Illinois or Kentucky. On balance, western coal appears to be a good deal, and the rapidly rising production statistics for the 1970s bear witness to its attractiveness (see table 3-1). Indeed,

Table 3–1. U.S. Coal Production, East and West of the Mississippi River, 1950–80

Year	West Million short tons	West Percentage of total	East Million short tons	East Percentage of total	United States
1950	36	6.4	524	93.6	560
1960	21	4.8	413	95.2	434
1970	45	7.3	568	92.7	613
1971	51	9.1	510	91.9	561
1972	64	10.6	538	89.4	602
1973	76	12.7	523	86.3	599
1974	92	15.1	518	84.9	610
1975	111	16.9	544	83.1	655
1976	136	19.9	549	80.1	685
1977	164	23.5	533	76.5	697
1978	183	27.3	487	72.7	670
1979	221	28.3	560	71.7	781
1980	251	30.1	584	69.9	835

Source: Energy Information Administration, *1980 Annual Report to Congress*, vol. II; *Data* (Washington, D.C., GPO, 1981).

western coal accounted for the entire growth in U.S. coal production between 1972 and 1977.

Clean Coal/Dirty Air

For those fearing competition from western coal, the 1977 revision of the Clean Air Act presented a golden opportunity to redress the balance in favor of eastern coal. The way to do it was to alter the prescription for emissions regulation. On behalf of U.S. senators from four eastern coal states (Pennsylvania, West Virginia, Ohio, and Indiana), an amendment was introduced in the House of Representatives that slightly altered the wording of that part of the act that specifies means of achieving the mandated sulfur dioxide emission level. There are instances—and this is a prime example—when one needs a fine-tuned instrument to spot what often seem only nuances to discover the ultimate objective. Instead of asking for standards to reflect "emission limitations achievable through the application of the best system of emission reduction," the House amendment specified standards that were to reflect "the degree of emission reduction achievable through the application of the best technological system of continuous emission reduction." A fine recent book by Ackerman and Hassler, *Clean Coal/Dirty Air*,[1] details this episode in brilliant fashion.

Now, as one discovers when inquiring of those in the know, "continuous" was known to all concerned to be the code word for "scrubbers," an expensive and somewhat ornery technology for removing sulfur from stack emissions. This provision was strengthened further by the language about "reduction" rather than limitation achievable through emission reduction, and by stressing "technological" means. Use of low-sulfur coal without scrubbing failed to satisfy those new criteria. Obviously, as was the aim of the new language, this was apt to diminish greatly the attractiveness of low-sulfur western coal. Even though it would still be cheaper to clean 0.9 percent sulfur coal than 2.5 percent sulfur coal, the big advantage of burning it without cleaning was lost.

There is no guesswork in any of this. The heart of the matter was quite bluntly spelled out in the 507-page House report that accompanied the legislation. It declares that the unamended legislation gives "a competitive advantage to those states with cheaper low-sulfur coal and creates a disadvantage for Mid-Western and Eastern states where predominantly higher-sulfur coals are available."[2] In so doing, the old standard-setting ran counter, the report states, to the declared policy of widening the range of available fuel sources and other goals.

Scrubbers for All

The amendment language was widely—and, on existing evidence, I believe correctly—thought to have been based on a compromise between eastern coal interests and clean air advocates. In order to placate the eastern coal interests and have them support a tough clean air policy, the "continuous cleaning" provision with its implicit penalty for western coal was inserted into the act. It was left to the Environmental Protection Agency to work out the details, but the details had to spell "scrubbers for all" if the language and intent of the legislation were to be satisfied.

Among those favoring the changes were not only eastern coal mines, the congressional spokespersons for eastern coal, and eastern railroads, but also much of the environmental movement. The environmentalist support was based heavily on its long-standing hostility to surface mining's obvious disruption of the landscape and the uncertainty that the landscape would—or sometimes even could—be appropriately restored.

A second consideration, although it does not seem to have figured specifically on this occasion, was the distaste for boomtowns, for which Gillette, Wyoming, serves as the horrid example. I would not go as far as saying that opposition to coal development west of the Mississippi is based on a general "western mystique," but certainly for some there exists the ideal of a pristine West as the last refuge from the uglifications perpetrated by society.

The net result of the decision is a national policy that imposes the wasteful practice of cleaning relatively sulfur-free western coal and that generally distorts choices between eastern and western coal that otherwise would result. The "eastern tilt" was widespread. The National Coal Policy Project, in which environmentalists played a large role, recommended that coal mining be concentrated east of the Mississippi River, where reclamation was easier, and that power plants should be sited near load-centers, again favoring eastern coal through the transportation advantage.[3] "This conclusion," a Project press release, dated February 9, 1978, stated, "supports President Carter's eastern tilt toward coal development." Indeed, it did. President Carter's objective as expressed in the 1977 National Energy Plan predicted "large production increases in the . . . Eastern and Midwest regions," and where "the required use of best available control technology for new power plants should stimulate even greater use of high-sulfur Midwestern and Eastern coal."[4] However, as the share of eastern coal continued to decline, it is arguable that the tilt did not seriously impair the growth of western coal.

Coal Slurry Pipelines

The battle to prevent the construction of coal slurry pipelines, especially from the Northern Plains, also acts as a brake on western coal development. The slurry idea would beat the high cost of railroad transportation by mixing coal with liquid—conventionally water, but conceivably other fluids—and pumping the mixture through pipelines to users.

The slurry pipeline struggle has obvious regional aspects to it, but regional interests do not explain the whole story. The opposition consists of the railroads, both eastern and western, and a great many interests, some largely agricultural, that share a concern over the loss of water. That is, many people object to shipping sizable quantities of water from water-scarce states in the West to water-rich states in the East or South (an argument that provoked the proposal of a dual pipeline, one carrying coal east and one carrying water west, but costs appear prohibitive).

Cost studies indicate that for very large volumes and over long distances pipelines can carry coal more cheaply than can above-ground transportation. Moreover, if one believes that high rates of inflation will continue, a pipeline with its large initial investment and low operating costs would have a further advantage. At least one pipeline venture has been working toward building a line over 1,000 miles long, from Wyoming to Arkansas, by securing transit rights in state after state despite railroad opposition and rail control of most rights-of-way. It does so largely by finding crossings in areas where the railroads own only the bed but not the subsurface, so that the pipeline can tunnel under the railroad bed. But the opposition generally has prevailed and restricted severely this opportunity for lower-cost coal shipments. The arena of this fight also was the Congress, which repeatedly has considered legislation to accord the right of eminent domain to pipeline companies so they could cross railroad lines. The legislation last was defeated in 1978.

Proceedings of the summer 1978 hearings contain lists of organizations supporting and opposing the slurry pipeline legislation. The list of advocates is dominated by utility companies, all the way from Boston Edison to Pacific Gas and Electric. A number of governors and legislators from states at both the origin and terminal of proposed pipelines are represented, along with the National Coal Association (as one might expect) and such major federal government departments as Energy and Transportation. The opponents' list is more diverse. Apart from the railroads, including railroad labor unions, it leans heavily on farming organizations and on Montana and Nebraska local organizations (again heavily oriented toward farming), and, most interestingly, a number of environmental organizations such as the Sierra Club, the Friends of the Earth, and the Izaak Walton League. Unsurprisingly, the United Mine Workers, presumably protecting the interests of eastern coal, also show up on this list of otherwise strange bedfellows.

The water issue doubtless loomed large in this controversy, and in that respect the regional dimension is clear—water-poor versus water-rich areas. But the matter was hopelessly entangled by other dimensions, most prominently by the fight against rising coal railroad rates, involving above all the Burlington Northern and Southern Pacific lines, and by the desire of the railroads nationwide to protect their coal trade and revenues against pipeline encroachments. Whether and to what degree eastern coal interests helped defeat the legislation is not evident from the record.

There is a good chance that those environmental organizations that joined the opposition indulged no more than an intuitive dislike of western coal development. Whatever the case, however, the victory is futile, almost Pyrrhic, in important respects. Denial of pipeline transportation merely leaves the transportation of whatever coal is produced to the railroads and the manifest environmental and safety problems that are associated with them (for example, dust, noise, accidents). Moreover, these problems will multiply in number and in intensity as traffic increases: some people have visions of local citizens darting across the railroad tracks in those few moments between thundering unit coal trains passing almost continuously through their communities.

Broader Issues

The initial public concentration on the physical aspects of the energy problem now is giving way to some broader economic and social issues. One of these relates to the relative shift in income and employment from energy-deficient to energy-surplus states and regions. A second involves more directly the uneven distribution of the burden among energy-users in different regions and states. Both of these sets of issues clearly are the sort of thing that people have in mind when they refer to increasing regional conflict within the United States.

The mere concept—let alone the quantitative determination—of energy-deficient and energy-surplus states is relatively new, at least in the sense of gaining importance. It is altogether likely, however, with oil price decontrol now a fact and natural gas price decontrol on the horizon, that it will assume great importance.

Two separate developments have helped focus attention on these aspects of energy. One has been the struggle of low-income households to meet their energy needs, and associated with it the regional differences that were discovered in the course of studying the problem and its remedies.[5] The other has been rising state revenues from taxation of energy production through severance and other taxes and royalty fees. Inasmuch as chapter 4 presents a much-discussed instance in the severance tax issue, the subject is treated here only in general fashion, followed by a more detailed exploration of energy-associated shifts in growth and of consumer expenditure problems.

Severance and Other Local Taxes

Two aspects of the tax issue seem particularly interesting. The first is how small the sums involved have been so far, compared with other income transfers, such as those associated with windfall profits on oil. The second is that some of these taxes have been around for a long time in more than half the states of the Union. Moreover, in their relationship to state revenues, they are far more significant in several states other than Montana, where the matter has come to a head not because of the nature of the tax but its magnitude. This fact may have persuaded Texas—which has the largest severance tax income of any state—to join the court case in opposition to Montana, as described in the next chapter.

From tables 3-2 and 3-3, which list state taxes and their significance, we see that Louisiana has a revenue tax on oil of 12.5 percent of gross value that provided nearly 24 percent of the state's revenues in 1978. Wyoming's taxes are 4, 4, and 17 percent (recently raised from 10.5 percent) on oil, natural gas, and coal, respectively, and in 1978 they provided nearly 23 percent of its revenues. Despite its 30 percent coal severance tax, Montana derives only 12 percent of its revenues from severance taxes. In absolute terms, these state revenues in 1979 ranged from as little as $26 million in North Dakota to over $1 billion in Texas, according to a study released by the National Academy of Sciences.[6]

These are not mind-boggling sums at a time when the nation as a whole spends some $150 billion on energy at the primary resource level, and in the neighborhood of more than twice as much at the end-use level. Thus, so far the argument has been more on principle than on any credible contention of heavy damage inflicted by these taxes. It is only the 1979–80 jump in the world price of oil followed by decontrol of the domestic market and the approaching decontrol of the price of most natural gas that make the taxing power of the energy-exporting states an apparent threat to energy-importing states.

An unpublished U.S. Treasury calculation, cited—and characterized as very preliminary and rough—by the Northeast–Midwest Institute (the research arm of the Northeast–Midwest Congressional Coalition), estimates that as a result of oil price decontrol state and local revenues will rise by more than $127 billion in the 1980s, 90 percent of which will accrue in the eight major oil-producing states.[7] Note, however, that this estimate is not limited to taxes on production, but encompasses all state revenues. Nonetheless, these begin to be large numbers. When one adds

Table 3–2. State Production Taxes on Coal, Oil, Natural Gas, as of 1979

State	Coal	Oil	Natural gas
Alabama	33.5¢	6%	—
Alaska	—	12.25%	10%
Arkansas	2.0¢	4–5%[ab] plus 0.5¢	3¢
California	—	[c]	[c]
Colorado	—	2–5%[d]	3–5%[d]
Florida	5%	8%	5%
Georgia	—	0.5¢	0.5¢
Idaho	2%	0.5¢	0.05¢
Indiana	—	1%	—
Kentucky	4.5%	0.5%[a]	—
Louisiana	10¢	12.5%[b]	7¢
Michigan	—	2%	2%
Mississippi	—	6¢ or 6%[e]	0.3¢ or 4%[e]
Montana	[f]	2.65%[g]	2.65%[g]
Nebraska	—	2%	2%
New Mexico	19.2¢[h] 40.5¢[i]	47.9¢	5.3¢
North Dakota	65¢	5%	5%
Ohio	4¢	3¢	1¢
Oklahoma	—	7.085%	7.085%
South Dakota	4.5%[j]	3%	3%
Tennessee	20¢	4.2¢	5%[k]
Texas	—	4.6[l]	7.5%
Utah	2%	2%	2%
Wyoming	10.5%[a]	4%	4%

Source: Committee on Energy Taxation, Assembly of Behavioral and Social Sciences, National Research Council, *Energy Taxation: An Analysis of Selected Taxes* (Washington, D.C., 1980).

[a] of market value
[b] varies with size of well
[c] varies from year to year; set by state legislature
[d] varies with size of gross revenue
[e] whichever greater
[f] greater of 12–40¢/tons or 20–30% of FOB mine price for surface and 5–12¢/ ton or 3–4% of FOB mine price for underground coal
[g] After 2.1% of gross of first $6,000 of gross value
[h] Metallurgical coal
[i] Underground coal
[j] of taxable value
[k] of sales price
[l] of value of oil selling in excess of $1/bbl

substantial, although not necessarily equally massive, revenues that will accrue when natural gas is decontrolled, it becomes clear that we are dealing with rather impressive magnitudes. No wonder energy-deficient states exhibit increasing concern and are trying to limit the damage by

Table 3–3. Severance Tax Revenues for Selected States, 1979
(in millions of dollars)

State	Revenues	Percentage of total state tax revenues
Alaska	173.7	21.2
Florida	91.9	2.1
Kentucky	154.0	7.4
Louisiana	496.4	22.2
Mississippi	30.7	2.5
Montana	52.4	11.1
New Mexico	155.8	18.5
North Dakota	25.5	7.9
Oklahoma	281.0	18.6
Texas	1,019.2	17.8
Wyoming	87.4	25.5

Source: Committee on Energy Taxation, Assembly of Behavioral and Social Sciences, National Research Council, *Energy Taxation: An Analysis of Selected Taxes* (Washington, D.C., 1980).

putting a legislative cap on tax rates—an attempt, incidentally, that if successful might rapidly turn the cap into the norm.

Core of the Controversy

What is it that most exercises these states? In the first place, it is the fact that accrual of large revenues to the energy-rich states enables them to keep other taxes down; for example, Texas and Wyoming have no personal or corporate income taxes. Obviously, a state without income taxes is attractive to both individuals and corporations. Rising oil and natural gas prices will further augment state revenues, further postpone the need for other taxes, and constitute a growing incentive for moving to locations that enjoy this particular position (although so far no great rush of people has been anxious to move to North Dakota or Utah, two of the few remaining states without a personal income tax).

Second, because of the particular way in which revenue-sharing and some other federal funds have been allocated, severance taxes not only do not diminish—as one might naively expect—a state's share of federal aid but indeed increase it. The relevant formulas contain a provision under which a state that "taxes itself" is considered worthy of an increased federal contribution. This would make sense if the taxes raised were to come out of the hides of the state's citizens. But, depending on market conditions, part of the severance taxes may be "exported," that is, be paid by citizens of other states. All in all, the preferential treatment in federal revenue-sharing formulas makes little sense. If exceedingly slack energy markets were to cause buyers to stay away from buying oil, natural gas, or coal from states that levy a severance or other excise tax on the energy product—a development not, for the moment, on the horizon—then the exporting state's citizens would indeed have to "eat" the tax. Formulated more generally, the extent to which such a tax can be imposed on out-of-state consumers or has to be absorbed by producers will depend on demand elasticity for the product from the given location, including the nature of contractual obligations.

Much has been made of threats by other states of imposing new or raising existing excise taxes, on agricultural crops, say, or on lumber. But in most instances, it is difficult to see how a single state finds itself in a demand and supply situation where it could impose a commodity tax without cutting significantly into out-of-state sales or encroaching on the income of its producers.

Thus, fears—featured on and off in news stories—that the nation is about to disintegrate into competitively taxing states seem wildly exaggerated,[8] simply because effective taxing capacity is severely circumscribed. But there is no denying that these taxes are an irritant even at their present level, and that in time the revenue-raising power of the major oil, gas, and to a lesser degree, coal states indeed could become large enough to constitute a real threat to the energy-deficient states.

Adding to the displeasure of the energy-poor states are threats beyond the tax burden—the higher cost of energy to consumers in these states, and loss of production and employment. To the extent these threats are real, they are, probably rightly, perceived as adding insult to injury by those states adversely affected by rising energy costs.

It is hard to say much with any assurance about shifts in population and economic activity because the evidence is insufficient for drawing firm conclusions. These macro events move slowly, and energy costs have been rising for only eight years, and then only in two distinct periods—1974 and 1979–80. Also, as discussed below, the moves one would anticipate by and large are in the same directions in which they have been going prior to the 1970s. Moreover, energy prices are important, but they are only one of many factors. So far, I have not seen data or analyses that suggest what has been due to price movements and what to other causes (such as, for example, the placement of federally funded activities).

Population Movements

Figures now available from the 1980 Census show a shift from the North and East toward the South and West, precisely what one would expect energy price movements to trigger. But when the 1970s are viewed in a longer time perspective, what appears to be distinct movement is merely a continuation of a trend that is many decades old. Charles Leven makes the point by calculating decadal population growth rates for the different regions (table 3-4).[9] Approaching the trend from a slightly different angle, figure 3-1 portrays the migration of the nation's population center. Both tests show a continuous basic western movement, but one tilted somewhat toward the South. Population growth in the Northeast has been the smallest among the four main regions in each of the last four decades, and that of the West the largest.

Thus, nothing really was new in 1970–80, with the small exception that the South was the only one of the four areas that experienced a larger rate of population growth in the 1970s than in the 1960s; this was especially pronounced in the West South Central Standard Federal Region, where the rate doubled from 1960–70 to 1970–80. The West South Central consists of Arkansas, Louisiana, Oklahoma, and Texas, that is, it contains three of the oil-and-gas-richest states. The only other region that strongly bucked the decline in the growth rate was the Mountain Region, which contains big coal producers Montana and Wyoming, as well as other states with significant energy resources—Colorado, New Mexico, and Utah. It is tempting to interpret these data as showing a correlation between energy endowment and population growth, but it is hazardous to draw conclusions from such large aggregates. I shall resist the temptation, but the reader may well ponder Leven's data as reproduced in table 3-4.

Table 3–4. Yearly Percentage of Population Growth by Region, 1940–80

Region	1940–50	1950–60	1960–70	1970–80
Northeast	1.09	1.56	1.01	− 0.01
North Central	1.56	1.76	1.06	0.33
South	2.61	2.59	1.38	1.75
West	3.75	3.50	2.37	2.08
United States	2.14	2.26	1.36	1.02

Source: Charles L. Leven, "Regional Shifts and Metropolitan Reversal in the U.S.," Paper presented at Conference on Urbanization and Development, June 1–4, 1981, International Institute for Applied Systems Analysis, Vienna, Austria, June 1981.

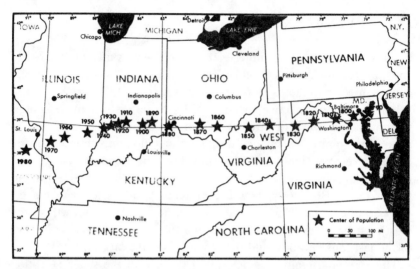

Figure 3–1. Geographic center of population:1790–1980. From U.S. Bureau of the Census, *Statistical Abstract of the United States, 1981* (Washington, D.C., 1981).

Shifts in Per Capita Income

What about income and employment? Obviously a potentially very divisive issue, it has not aroused as much discussion and controversy as one might have expected. The reasons for this, I believe, are similar to those mentioned with regard to shifts in economic activity: such shifts occur too slowly to be reflected in as brief a period as 1974 to 1980; increases in real energy prices to users have not been steady, but have come in two jumps, with a plateau in between; energy prices are only one among many factors that cause production and employment to shift among states, and whatever statistical devices one can apply to detect shifts at best are only suggestive of the specific role that energy prices may have played.

With these cautions, I refer to some calculations presented by William Miernyk in a paper Resources for the Future commissioned for a conference on the distributional aspects of rising energy costs.[10] Dividing the states into those that produce as much as or more energy than they consume, those that produce at least half but not all of the energy they consume, and those that produce less than half, Miernyk identifies twelve surplus states, thirty-one deficit states (producing less than 50 percent of their consumption), and seven states in between (50 to 100 percent self-sufficient). Incidentally, the twelve surplus states account for only 14 percent of the U.S. population; not counting Texas would shrink that percentage to just 8 percent. That is to say, the energy-surplus states represent a relatively small minority when it comes to voting in the Congress. But that is another matter.

Another characteristic of this division is that only two of the surplus states—Kentucky and West Virginia—lie east of the Mississippi. Thus, the "haves" basically are in the West, and especially the Southwest, and the "have-nots" in the East and the North Central region. The question that arises is whether the energy-surplus states have shown a greater than average growth in, say, income and employment, such as might result from higher prices of oil, natural gas, and coal, from rising coal production, and from steeply rising oil and gas exploration and development. Such events would not only raise local individual and corporate incomes, but also would attract secondary business and employment. Of course, not all income from energy activities accrues to recipients residing in the state. This is eminently true of corporate income that may be paid out in any number of ways and locations.

Long-term statistics on per capita income by standard federal regions are a useful indicator (figure 3-2). As noted in chapter 2, the overall finding is that regional deviations from the national per capita average have diminished, or, put differently, per capita income levels are converging toward the national average. The Northeast, where per capita income historically has been high, has lost ground, and the Midwest and South have gained. The narrowing of the spread is striking. While in 1929 it ranged from 50 percent below (Region IV, basically the old South) to 50 percent above (Region I, New England) the U.S. average; by 1979, Region IV, still the poorest, was less than 20 percent below the average and the richest, Region IX (California, Nevada, Arizona, and Hawaii) was only about 15 percent above it. An extraordinary shrinkage of differences indeed.

In the energy context of the 1970s it is of some interest to find that Region I (New England) declined sharply (but so it did from 1930 to 1950), and that Region VIII (the western coal states) sharply reversed the declining trend of the preceding decade, but so did Region VII (basically the midwestern grain states). Region VI, the southwestern oil and natural gas states, also showed a steep rise, accentuating a somewhat less steep increase in the preceding decade. In addition to Region I,

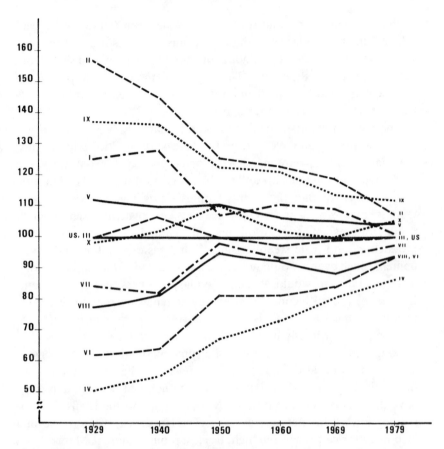

Figure 3–2. Regional per capita income as a percentage of U.S. average 1929–79 (Standard Federal Regions). From William Miernyk, "The Differential Effects of Rising Energy Prices on Regional Income and Employment," in Hans H. Landsberg, ed., *High Energy Costs: Assessing the Burden* (Washington, D.C., Resources for the Future, 1982) p. 306.

Region V—the midwestern and Great Lakes states—also worsened its position, accelerating the decline it had suffered in the 1960s. Figure 3-3, taken from Miernyk's paper, shows the full story. The suggestion that energy endowment may have something to do with per capita income trends is sharpened when individual states are identified. The sharp upward movement for such states as Texas, Oklahoma, Louisiana, West Virginia, and Wyoming, contrasts graphically with the downward movements for states like New York, Massachusetts, New Jersey, and others.

Yet, the shoe does not always fit. For example, the Midwest—one of the gainers—does not include a single one of the energy-surplus states; indeed, it is the most compact energy-deficient area. And of the two western regions, only Alaska ranks among the surplus states, so that energy endowment hardly can be responsible for the upward trend in their per capita income. Second, to the extent that the shoe does fit, as in the southern region, the differences in trend are not very pronounced. And third, there simply are too many factors involved to permit one to single out any one as *the* cause, or even the dominant one.

I am not certain what to make of these data. Surely it is tempting to make the connection with energy, as it is both plausible and mildly persuasive when one looks only at the past two decades. But viewed against the longer trend, when energy hardly was a big factor (in the sense of the past eight years), one is inclined to abandon the hypothesis and instead look for a different set of variables. It is not quite like reading tea leaves, but neither does the exercise inspire confidence, and for the moment I am content to leave it there, with one qualification. Now that controls on the price of domestic oil have ended and those on natural gas will come off, at least partially, within the next four years at the most, energy *prices* will begin to give added weight to local differences in energy *endowment*. Thus, the matter bears watching and calls for a substantially more profound analysis than so far has been given it, including prominently an investigation of whether regions are sufficiently homogeneous to serve as basic units of observation. This is especially important if one employs the popular Snowbelt and Sunbelt terminology and equates it with energy-poor and energy-rich states. As noted in chapter 2, this equation simply does not hold, which is not, alas, the same thing as saying that it is likely to impede the flow of calculations cast in broad terms.

Differential Impact on Consumers

To what extent has the fact that energy consumers as individuals or households have been affected unevenly by the rising cost of heating oil, gasoline, natural gas, and electricity, given rise to regional jealou-

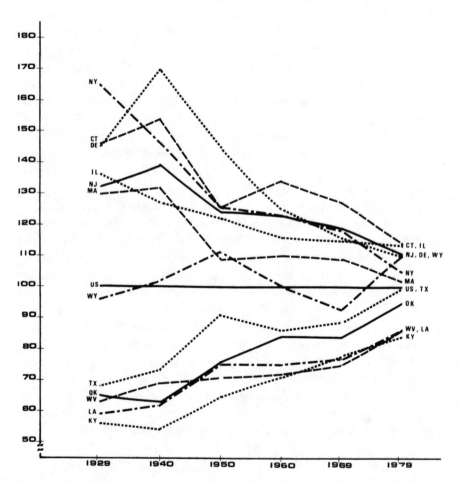

Figure 3–3. Relative per capita income in selected energy-surplus and energy-deficit states, 1929–79. From William Miernyk, "The Differential Effects of Rising Energy Prices on Regional Income and Employment," in Hans H. Landsberg, ed., *High Energy Costs: Assessing the Burden* (Washington, D.C., Resources for the Future, 1982) p. 308.

sies? It is conventional wisdom, for example, that northeasterners, and especially New Englanders, have been especially hard hit, a judgment that frequently results in a demand for remedial legislation aimed especially at those parts of the country. There is truth to it, but it is complicated, and requires a look at the past as well as the present. What seem to be the facts?[11]

I shall limit myself to two sources of data. One is the special energy consumer survey that was undertaken by the Department of Energy in the twelve-month period between April 1978–March 1979, that is, just prior to the big price push that followed the 1979 OPEC oil price boost. The other is material put together from DOE's *State Energy Data Report* by the Northeast–Midwest Institute. The former data are useful because they differentiate among energy *sources,* but they do not permit comparison with other years, nor are they available for any but residential consumers. The second set offers data for 1970, 1978, and, by extrapolation, 1980, and distinguishes between prices for different *classes* of users, but not fuel *sources.*

Regional Differences

To begin with the first, table 3-5 shows clearly that during the survey period households in the Northeast and North Central census regions faced considerably higher prices than did those in the South and West. This is most pronounced for electricity, for which the Northeast pays 85 percent higher rates than does the West (where cheap hydro power holds down the average). For natural gas, the Northeast pays nearly 50 percent more. Regional price differences are small for fuel oil and ker-

Table 3–5. Average Prices of Residential Energy Sources Delivered to User—Nationwide and by Census Region, April 1978–March 1979 (dollars per million Btus)

Regional	Electricity	Natural gas	Fuel oil and kerosine	Liquefied petroleum gas
Nationwide	$12.10	$2.74	$3.93	$5.09
Northeast	15.34	3.42	3.98	7.93
North Central	13.64	2.57	3.82	4.55
South	11.75	2.85	3.94	5.16
West	8.28	2.30	3.77	4.18

Source: Residential Energy Consumption Survey: Consumption and Expenditures, April 1978 Through March 1979, DOE/EIA–0207/5 (Washington, D.C., DOE/EIA, July 1980) table 3.

osine, as is true for most petroleum products; the major exception is bottled gas, which costs 50 to 90 percent more in the Northeast than in the other regions.

While costs for electricity are highest in the Northeast, the North Central states do not fare much better. On the positive side, North Central residents enjoy relatively low-priced natural gas, with only the West paying less for it. All in all, price differentials at the user's level are substantial and in general favor the South and West which, by and large, are the energy-surplus states.

In interpreting these figures one must take into account that the magnitude of the burden is a function not only of price, but also of the quantities of the particular energy source consumed. For example, the fact that high transportation costs make natural gas expensive in New England loses significance when one realizes that New England's energy mix is lean on gas; and it is lean precisely because it is expensive, relative both to other regions and to other energy sources. For example, in the Northeast natural gas costs only 14 percent less than fuel oil, whereas it costs between 30 and 40 percent less elsewhere. Thus, a major disadvantage in the Northeast is the minor importance of nationally inexpensive natural gas, and the relatively high price of it when northeastern consumers do use it, the high price being largely a function of distance from the source.

Differences among individual states, rather than regions, are even more striking. Thus, residential natural gas consumers in 1978 paid $5.40 per 1 million Btus in Maine, while Oklahomans paid $1.88 and Arkansans $1.67. Rates for industrial consumers were lower across the board, but differentials were found to be nearly as large. The lowest state average price in 1978 (leaving aside Alaska) was $1.27 in Wyoming, and the highest (leaving aside Hawaii) was $3.33 in Maine; the more industry-intensive New York–New Jersey area average, at $2.50–$2.80, ranged toward the high end of the spread.[12]

Changes Over Time

A look at the dynamics of these differentials rounds out the picture. It is one thing to find they exist at a given time and quite another to find they have been changing. Here comparisons are of the total energy package, that is, the average cost of a package of energy, however composed, compared in 1970 and 1980. The relevant data are shown in

Table 3–6. Average Energy Prices, by Region, for 1970 and 1980

(dollars per billion Btus)

Region	1970	1980	Percentage increase 1970–80
Residential			
Northeast	1,598	5,808	263
Midwest	1,430	4,388	207
South	1,411	4,136	193
West	1,098	3,603	228
United States	1,403	4,472	219
Industrial			
Northeast	847	4,256	402
Midwest	723	3,130	333
South	462	2,795	505
West	651	3,167	386
United States	628	3,166	403

Source: *National and State Energy Expenditures 1970–1980* (Washington, D.C., Northeast–Midwest Institute, July 1981).

table 3-6.[13] Again, the situation for residential consumers is worst in the Northeast. For them, the average price paid per 1 million Btus (from all sources) jumped 263 percent, compared with a jump of "only" 193 percent in the South and a national average increase of 219 percent.

Essentially the same differential pattern held for commercial users, whereas for industrial and transportation energy users the Northeast was in step with the national average. Indeed, for industrial users it was the South that experienced a relative increase in energy prices far above the national average. This raises an important issue, often ignored. In 1970, the statistics show that industrial energy prices in the South were 26 percent below the national average; in 1980 that differential had shrunk to 12 percent. Clearly, those areas that had enjoyed especially low prices were catching up to the national average. This development illustrates how misleading it can be to look merely at differentials at a point in time: it may be much more punishing for the prosperity of an area with low energy prices to suffer drastic boosts, while still remaining *below* the national average, than for a high-cost area to undergo moderate boosts and still stay *above* the national average. It is the first situation that appears to prevail for energy price changes for industrial users in the South, but it will not show if one uses a snapshot approach.

Table 3–7. Residential Energy Expenditures Per Household, for 1970 and 1980 (in millions of dollars)

Region	1970	1980	Percentage increase
Northeast	338	1,138	237
Midwest	367	1,150	213
South	288	896	211
West	263	676	157
United States	315	963	206

Source: *National and State Energy Expenditures 1970–1980* (Washington, D.C., Northeast–Midwest Institute, July 1981).

Household Differences

Prices per unit of energy are not the whole story. Energy expenditures per household (or commercial or industrial customer, for that matter) complete the analysis. As one might expect, the Northeast and Midwest are at the high end, and the South and West at the low end of the expenditure range, both in terms of comparisons at one time and in terms of increases in the 1970s. In both respects the differences are substantial (table 3-7).

Broad regional aggregates mask even bigger state-by-state differences. To cite two extremes, the average household in the state of Washington paid $242 for its energy in 1970 and an estimated $501 ten years later. A Maine resident paid $382 in 1970, and $1,449 in 1980. In other words, the Maine homeowner paid 60 percent more than the Washingtonian in 1970, and nearly 200 percent more in 1980.

A look back at the energy consumption pattern in 1972, as displayed in abundant detail in Irving Hoch's study on regional energy statistics,[14] explains the greater impact on the Northeast and some parts of the Midwest and Mid-Atlantic states since the 1972 data were compiled. Limiting our field of vision to New England, we find that household energy consumption accounted for 43 percent of the total energy consumption in 1972, as against 16 percent, for example, in the West South Central, and 28 percent nationally. Moreover, in New England 80 percent of all energy use in 1972 consisted of petroleum products, compared with 40 percent nationwide (and 27 percent in the West South Central region); for household consumption alone the differences are even more dramatic.

What it comes down to—again using Hoch's data—is that in New England per capita heating fuel use was three times the national average and nine times the per capita use in the West. Add to this information the fact that the price (per gallon) of residential heating oil jumped from 19.7 cents in 1972 to 97.8 cents in 1980—or by nearly 400 percent—compared with a rise in the Consumer Price Index only about half as steep, and the elements and dimensions of the regional equity issue begin to emerge clearly.

To summarize, the point is not that northeasterners were especially hard hit just because the price of heating oil rose steeply; it did so everywhere. Rather, they were hard hit because they use more energy for space conditioning and are so much more dependent on fuel oil than on natural gas that was both cheaper to start with and, being a regulated commodity, rose much less rapidly in price. Thus, northeasterners were triply penalized: they use more energy; they had to rely on the more expensive energy source, fuel oil; and that source's price rose faster than that of its closest competitor, natural gas. To make matters worse, houses in that part of the country generally are older and harder to heat. This mattered less before the 1970s, but it matters greatly now. The charm of a century-old frame house is greatly diminished by a monthly $200 or $300 bill from the local fuel oil dealer.

Today's Winners, Tomorrow's Losers?

I have singled out fuel oil and the Northeast because that is where the problem is most graphic. For gasoline, the Northeast may well have a relative advantage, because it is more heavily urban and relatively more compact. Also, much of it was built in the preautomobile age and therefore has more mass transportation facilities. As for electricity, while its costs are highest in the Northeast, reliance on it is far less than in parts of the country where it is cheap and where it has made large gains in space-heating. Some states, predominantly those whose energy mix has a large hydroelectricity component (for example, Washington and Idaho) have been able to hold the line on price with some success; but it is almost certain that rates in such states will begin rising more sharply as new nonhydro capacity is brought on-line. When the state of Washington, for instance, succeeds finally in bringing some new nuclear power plants on-line, the costs per kilowatt hour are bound to take a giant leap, given the enormous cost overruns in construction so far; and anyone following events in the Tennessee Valley Authority area must be impressed by the traumatic nature of each increase—and there have been more than one—in electricity rates.

I cite these instances merely as examples of the fluidity of the situation: this year's winners in the price lottery may well be tomorrow's losers. Nonetheless, the present handicap of the northeastern fuel oil-dependent states is undeniable and explains the special sense of injury that emanates from their political representatives. This mind-set, of course, is not unknown in parts of the Midwest and Mid-Atlantic. As an example, the Northeast–Midwest Congressional Coalition published a booklet that bears the title "The United American Emirates," a phrase that can take its place alongside its older cousin, the "blue-eyed Arabs," variously applied to Canadians, Montanans, and other energy-rich North Americans.

Coming increases in the price of natural gas, following decontrol, and of electricity, as high-cost capacity is put in service, will begin to squeeze portions of the country that so far have felt the price pinch less. I am inclined, therefore, to believe that regional friction, including name-calling, not only will not increase, but indeed may diminish later in the decade. Misery will not *seek* company, but it is nonetheless likely to get it. As regional price and expenditure differentials shrink, complaints from the South and West will match and offset those now heard from the Northeast and Midwest.

How Serious a Problem?

Evaluations of different aspects of conflict based on data of greatly varying quality are difficult to meld into an overall judgment of how serious a problem we have before us. Regional shifts in population and in economic activity as reflected in per capita income are both slow and hard to ascribe to rising energy prices or any other particular cause. So far, at least, the evidence is far from compelling. The uneven distribution of the cost burden on consumers in different parts of the country is well-documented, but my guess is that this situation will be attenuated as other prices catch up with those of the petroleum products.

The conflicts over which coal resources to develop are real and have been so for a number of years. At most, however, they may have slowed western coal growth, certainly not stopped it. Legislation and regulation effectively mandating scrubbers for all have made pollution control more costly and difficult and added to the cost of electricity. They present a fascinating chapter in law-making and an interesting case study of the formation of "odd coalitions." But they are not the kind of thing from which severe and sustained regional conflict springs.

This leaves as a major irritant substantial and growing differences in state revenues between states that can and do tax energy production within their borders, and are able to shift payments to consumers elsewhere, and those that are in no such position. Severance taxes are the prime example. Even though the amounts are not presently large on a national scale or in terms of the price of energy to the final consumer, and even though there is good reason to doubt that states can in fact pass forward to consumers in other states a major part of any of the taxes they impose, the concept itself has aroused much hostility. It can and probably will lead to a good deal of mischief, as means of retaliation are sought and found, such as New York's and Connecticut's attempts to tax oil companies with headquarters in their territory. The present state of affairs does not justify exaggerated headlines. Not yet. But it is cause for concern to see one more divisive element join the many that already make the forming of consensus in our society so difficult a venture.

Most likely to arouse passion are dramatic fiscal steps taken by individual states, such as in the potentially explosive case of severance or other production excise taxes, or specific site-connected conflicts, such as nuclear waste disposal, rapidly rising coal railroad traffic, with its adverse effect on those living alongside the tracks, or the unequal impact of burdens imposed by offshore oil and gas development. To the extent that such activities can be engineered and operated to be less offensive to those physically close to them, regional friction will be reduced. But, beyond this, the nation should be careful that in trying to soften impacts we do not significantly impede shifts in economic activity, including those of population, employment, and investment. Such shifts are the appropriate response to differentially changing prices and availability of energy resources. They are the hallmark of a well-functioning market economy that takes its cues from prices and does not like to be fooled.

Notes

1. Bruce A. Ackerman and William T. Hassler, *Clean Coal/Dirty Air* (New Haven, Conn., Yale University Press, 1981).

2. U.S. House of Representatives, *Clean Air Act Amendments of 1976, Report to the Committee on Interstate and Foreign Commerce*, May 15, 1978, 94th Cong., 2d sess., Report No. 94-1175, p. 160.

3. National Coal Policy Project, *Where We Agree*, Report of the National Coal Policy Project, vol. II, sect. 2, I, (Boulder, Colo., Westview Press, 1978) pp. 33–67.

4. Executive Office of the President, *The National Energy Plan* (Washington, D.C., GPO, April 1977).

5. Energy assistance in cash did not really exist in any substantial degree until FY 1980 when Congress appropriated $1.6 billion for that purpose, in addition to $200 million for weatherization assistance.

6. National Research Council–National Academy of Sciences, *Energy Taxation: An Analysis of Selected Taxes*, Report of the Committee on Energy Taxation, National Research Council–National Academy of Sciences (Washington, D.C., 1980).

7. Northeast–Midwest Institute, *The Effects of Rising State Severance Tax Revenues 1980–1990*, Regional Energy Impact Brief No. 10 (Washington, D. C., Northeast–Midwest Institute, April 1980) p. 5. Much higher figures can—and have been—concocted by making necessary assumptions with respect to future oil, gas, and coal prices and supplies.

8. "War Between the States," *Time* Magazine, August 21, 1981; "A New Civil War Looms Over State Taxes on Natural Resources," *The Washington Post*, August 19, 1981. Politicians have joined the fray, namely, Gov. Brendon Byrne (N.J.) cited in a *Time* magazine article as saying: "It is potentially the largest transfer of wealth in the history of the United States," matched only by *Time's* own observation: "Perhaps the most important test for the Union since the Civil War."

9. Charles L. Leven, "Regional Shifts and Metropolitan Reversal in the U.S." Paper presented at Conference on Urbanization and Development, International Institute for Applied Systems Analysis, Vienna, Austria, June 14, 1981.

10. See Hans H. Landsberg and Joseph M. Dukert, *High Energy Costs: Uneven, Unfair, Unavoidable?* (Baltimore, Md., The Johns Hopkins University Press for Resources for the Future, 1981), and *High Energy Costs: Assessing the Burden. Proceedings of a Conference Organized by Resources for the Future and the Brookings Institution, October 9–10, 1980* (Washington, D.C., Resources for the Future, 1982).

11. For a detailed exposition of the facts and problems, see Landsberg and Dukert, *High Energy Costs*, p. 23.

12. Ibid., pp. 95–96.

13. Derived from Northeast–Midwest Institute, *National and State Energy Expenditures 1970-1980*, (Washington, D.C., July 1981).

14. Irving Hoch, *Energy Use in the United States by State and Region* (Washington, D.C., Resources for the Future, 1978).

chapter four

Typical Cases Involving Natural Resources

Allen V. Kneese

Many regional conflicts involve what economists call *external effects* or *externalities*. In the present context, these occur when a state (or states), possibly through the medium of the federal government, imposes a cost (or a benefit) on another state or states in which the recipient state does not have direct control over that imposition. Externalities may be *real*, meaning that the effect is directly through a natural medium, such as interstate river pollution, or *pecuniary*, as when one state can impose monetary costs on another state, say, by its tax policy or through political pressure. Salinity in the Colorado River, which will be examined shortly, has both of these features. The upstream states impose real external costs on the downstream states, because their activities cause salinity to increase in the river, and both impose similar costs on Mexico. But the international dimension, plus the traditional politics of the region, permit the upstream and downstream states to resolve their differences and impose a pecuniary external cost on the rest of the country. There also is the further question of why the United States would agree to reduce the salinity going to Mexico when apparently it has nothing to gain from such a reduction.

Economic rents are created in the exploitation of many natural resources. Because of superior quality, including locational aspects, some
resources may be exploitable at a cost well below that of other otherwise
similar resources that also are in the market. Economists call the difference the economic rent of the resource deposit—the amount by which
costs of exploitation could rise without making it unprofitable to continue the operation. Such a rent is a tempting plum that different parties
may seek to pluck. The owners of the site may appropriate it, but it
also tempts the state where the site occurs because the deposit and its
qualities are immobile and, therefore, the rent can be extracted without
altering the activities of the operation or facing the threat of its moving
elsewhere. The particular case that I will treat briefly in this chapter is
Montana's state severance tax on coal. In this instance, most of the coal
is exported, and ownership of the coal companies is almost wholly outside the state. The opportunity exists, therefore, to benefit the citizens
of Montana at the expense of persons elsewhere in the country.

The third case to be explored is where a state perceives itself to be
required to bear unwarranted costs "in the national interest" and where
it regards itself as not being properly represented in the decision process.
This squarely involves Tenth Amendment or states' rights issues. The
particular instance I will describe involves the proposed nuclear waste
repository, the Waste Isolation Pilot Plant (WIPP), near Carlsbad, New
Mexico.

Salinity in the Colorado River

Salinity is a disease—sometimes a fatal one—that afflicts irrigation and
other activities in most arid basins. Salt springs, salt leached from earth
and rock, and salt in return-flow irrigation water all contribute to the
load, but the main contribution in recent years to increased salinity in
the lower Colorado Basin is the higher concentration of salts resulting
from increased use of the relatively pure water of the upper basin, mainly
in interbasin diversions. This results in less dilution of the salt load on
the river and therefore higher salinity in the downstream areas.[1]

The headwaters of the Colorado River in Colorado contain a maximum of about 50 parts per million (ppm) of inorganic salts. By the time
the water reaches Imperial Valley irrigation in California, the salt con-

centration has reached about 870 ppm. This is still quite usable water, but the increased salinity causes substantial costs in the lower basin not only to irrigated crops, but also, through increased corrosion, to water conveyance and handling facilities. The Colorado River Compact, which in 1922 divided up the waters of the Colorado between the upper and the lower basin states, was silent on the salinity question, thus setting the stage for regional conflict on this issue.

The Mexican Issue

The United States completed a Colorado River treaty in 1944 with Mexico. The most important provision was an allotment to Mexico of a guaranteed annual quantity of water from the river of 1.5 million acre-feet per year (an acre-foot is the amount of water it would take to cover an acre to a depth of one foot). This treaty too said nothing about water quality.

For most of the period since 1944, the water delivered to Mexico, stored in Morelos reservoir, was not much worse than that delivered to users in the lower basin in the United States. Nevertheless, in the course of time the inevitable gradual reduction of water quality most probably would have caused salinity to arise as an international issue.

But in the early 1960s the quality of water being delivered to Mexico fell dramatically. In 1947 the Bureau of Reclamation's Wellton–Mohawk Project in southwestern Arizona was authorized by Congress to deliver water for the irrigation of 75,000 acres. As a solution to salinity problems the project encountered, in 1961 the Wellton–Mohawk irrigation district started pumping from drainage wells and discharging saline water into the Colorado River below the last U.S. diversion point, but above the Mexican diversion point. This water—with a salinity of about 6,000 ppm—jumped the salinity of the water delivered to Mexico from about 800 ppm in 1960 to more than 1,500 ppm in 1962. The effect of the increased salinity discharge was reinforced when the Glen Canyon Dam commenced filling in 1961 and the quantity of water delivered to Mexico dropped sharply. Mexico complained loudly.

Following some interim activities to try to blunt the issue, in August 1972 President Nixon appointed Herbert Brownell, Jr., as his special representative on the salinity problem with Mexico and assigned to him the job of finding a "permanent" solution. After delivering a report,

Brownell was appointed special ambassador to negotiate a solution with Mexico, the result of which was incorporated in Minute 242 of the International Water and Boundary Commission. This minute refers to itself as the "permanent and definitive solution" to the international salinity problem.

The Nixon administration pledged itself to undertake the following measures:

1. Construction of a major desalting plant and related works for Wellton–Mohawk drainage waters, scheduled to be completed by December 1978
2. Extension of the Wellton–Mohawk drain (for the brine from the plant) to the Gulf of California, to be completed by December 1976
3. Lining or construction of a new Coachella Canal in California, to be completed in April 1977
4. Improved Wellton–Mohawk irrigation efficiency, scheduled for completion by December 1978.

As part of the negotiations, the basin states put forward a proposed Colorado River Basin Salinity Control Program which included, but went beyond, the works that were required specifically by Minute 242. The program included facilities for controlling salinity at various points above Imperial Dam for the benefit of users in the United States as well as Mexico. It specified such measures as capping salt springs and diverting streams away from particular areas where heavy salt leaching occurs.

The U.S. Congress approved essentially the entire package. While behind schedule and somewhat scaled down from its original capacity, the desalting plant is going forward and is now scheduled for completion in 1986. Some other measures required by provisions of Minute 242, such as canal lining, have been completed.

Two questions are of special interest in the present context: What position did the states take in this situation of potentially increased conflict in the upstream-downstream portions of the basin, and already intense international conflict over the same issue? And, why did the United States agree to Minute 242 when all of its direct benefits are in Mexico and all of its costs are in the United States?

What the States Did

The negotiators for the United States apparently understood the character of water politics in the Southwest very well. Herbert Brownell made the following statement after the agreement had been reached:

> This is a project that is based on dollars and not on water. I told the Western States at the beginning of the negotiations that nothing would be done, and nothing has been done as a result of this agreement, which would adversely affect the orderly development of the Western States. There are no limitations in the agreement which would adversely affect any of the planned programs for the development of natural resources of the basin States.[2]

This statement reflects the assumption on the part of the negotiators that any politically successful agreement would have to come at little or no cost—either in terms of money or water—to those directly affected. Political scientists who study these issues refer to western water politics as "distributive." According to a leading expert, Dean Mann, among their main features are:

- Settlement of conflicts through coalition-building at the local and regional levels before going to the federal level
- Avoidance of confrontation among competing interests, as a result of which winners and losers in the political battle and income consequences are disguised
- Dependence on federal financing
- Logrolling for mutual benefit with other similarly situated interests who seek diverse objectives through congressional action.[3]

Mann goes on to say about the salinity program:

> . . . Traditional water politics appears to be leading to solutions congruent with the output of previous water politics, i.e., formation of a strong local or regional coalition by a process of bargaining and accommodation, leadership provided by federal bureaus, an ability to find a basis for bargaining with other interests—in this case, the national Administration—and an avoidance of issues that might make clear the winner and losers in the political battle. The achievement of unity within the entire basin has made the salinity control coalition a powerful one indeed. It has been successful thus far in achieving an approach

to the solution of the salinity problem that promises extensive benefits to traditional beneficiaries of such an approach with very little cost.

One might agree with the National Academy of Sciences in their view that water management on the Colorado River should reflect comprehensive assessments of alternatives and explicit recognition of trade-offs in the uses to which the river's water is put and the investments that make those investments possible. But the existing political arrangements and practices—based on complex constitutional, legal, administrative, and financial arrangements—make such analysis difficult. The consequence is planning by bargaining and decisions that are made possible because there is little or no sacrifice by any important interest within the region. Thus, intraregional trade-offs of costs and benefits are ignored while the general taxpayer pays the bill. Unfortunately, at the national level there is seldom a careful assessment of whether paying that bill compares favorably with paying other bills that might realize greater national welfare in return for the investment.[4]

The international aspect is the main difference between the political situation in this case and other notable water developments in the Southwest (for example, the Colorado Basin Project Act negotiated during the 1950s and 1960s, which sprinkled project authorizations around the basin). Using this aspect to argue successfully that reducing and controlling salinity in the Colorado was a national obligation, the states were able to shift the cost to the national taxpayer. At the same time, they were able to suppress a developing internal conflict between the upper and lower basin states by means of the Colorado Basin Salinity Program, again at the expense of the national taxpayer.

But why did the United States want so badly to enter into an agreement with Mexico from which all the visible benefits accrue to Mexico?

Why the United States Did It

In a situation like this, if one views the matter from a narrow economic point of view, no basis for agreement exists unless the victim country compensates the damaging country for costs incurred to reduce the damage. If the damaging country acts in its own immediate economic self-interest, it will not be willing to reach any other sort of agreement.

The Rhine River provides an interesting illustration of a situation that produces the victim-pays result. The Netherlands, being at the terminus of that river, stands in somewhat the same relation to the upstream countries as Mexico does to the United States on the Colorado. Indeed, salinity is the major water quality problem in both cases. The Dutch, finding it increasingly difficult to use the Rhine's waters either for industrial or municipal purposes, agreed in 1972 to pay the French, whose potash industry is the main source of Rhine salinity, 35 percent of the costs of control to reduce the salinity of the river.

But the United States has agreed to pay the *entire* cost of mitigating the Colorado situation. If the United States had narrowly interpreted its economic self-interest, it either would have done nothing or would have required Mexico to pay some or all of the costs of mitigation. This, then, leads one to wonder what factors, other than magnitudes and distribution of strictly economic costs and benefits, could be important in the U.S. decision. Economic costs and benefits, of course, always are pertinent to the development of national decisions, including this one. But if they had been the only consideration, the situation never would have turned out the way it did.

It appears that negotiations about international rivers frequently involve considerations in quite other arenas, and these "extraneous" considerations often are dominant. In other words, it is impossible to understand the outcome of such an international negotiation simply by looking at its apparent focus. Indeed, it may be that even the initiation of negotiations on an international river problem is spurred by noneconomic national interests; clearly the results often are. For example, John V. Krutilla has shown that various considerations, including military strategic ones, persuaded U.S. agreement to a treaty on the Columbia that was quite unfavorable to the United States economically.[5] Thus, matters such as trade concessions, military bases, and the desire to win allies in international politics often may be overriding considerations.

In addition, the international image a country wishes to project may be important. One might so interpret the agreement of the Swiss, who are at the head of the Rhine River, to pay 5 percent of the costs of reducing salt discharges in France. And a country may wish to demonstrate respect for international law, which holds that a polluting country is responsible for controlling its degradations of an international environmental medium. My own belief, however, is that these international good citizenship considerations are not nearly so important as those more directly concerning national self-interest.

Thus, the results of domestic and international conflicts between states and regions may not be so arbitrary or irrational as it first might seem. Indeed, as long as all interested parties have something of value to trade, and as long as national self-interest is the primary motive force in international affairs, as I believe it is, this broad trading process seems to be the only sure path to international agreements. This may be especially true in the situation that characterizes the salinity problem of the Colorado River.[6]

The 1973 agreement seems to have been a situation in which the United States was anxious to cultivate more favorable relations with Latin American countries and, more generally, to reduce international stresses in the world at large. But it is very interesting to observe the means the United States chose for implementing the agreement. In this connection, Irving Fox and coauthors have identified a number of premises about international agreements on rivers.[7] Their Premise No. 4 reads as follows: "Configuration of power and influence within a country may have an important bearing on the kind of program acceptable to it and upon how the planning and implementation of the program can be done effectively." Examples of such internal forces affecting the nature of agreements reached can be found in negotiations between the United States and Canada both on the Saint Lawrence and the Columbia. In both cases, regional interests had a powerful influence on the specific nature of the agreements reached.

The internal forces are especially clear in the salinity agreement. As suggested, the basin states seem to have been determined not to lose a single drop of water to Mexico, no matter what it might cost the general taxpayer in the United States. Rough calculations indicate that it would have been far cheaper to buy the necessary water rights to send purer water to the Mexicali Valley than to implement the means actually chosen, especially the desalting plant. But there simply was no effective advocate for efficiency, and the result is a wildly uneconomic approach to the problem of reducing salinity in the Mexicali Valley.[8]

The diplomatic language characteristic of international negotiations terms the agreement a "definitive and final solution" to the problem. Perhaps typically, however, a little space exists between the diplomatic language and the realities of the situation. Most important, further increases in salinity of the Colorado River are inevitable. In due course this will raise the question of what absolute levels of salinity are permitted to be delivered to Mexico (the agreement's relative prescription links the permitted deliveries of salt to what arrives at the Imperial Dam in the United States). The issue will rise again.

Does "Distributive Politics" Have a Future in the Southwest?

The great salinity negotiation involving the United States, Mexico, and each of the basin states may be the last exercise in distributive politics related to water in the Colorado Basin, at least on anything like such a scale. The remaining large water development projects—the Central Arizona Project and the Central Utah Project—are well on the way to completion, and the problem for the region is fast becoming one of allocating and using the fixed water supply efficiently. The only future development that might open up the distributive politics game on an even larger—if not grandiose—scale is the possibility of massive inter-basin transfers of water. Schemes that have been suggested range from relatively modest proposals, such as bringing 1 million acre-feet per year from the Snake River to the headwaters of the Colorado, to a gigantic proposal known as the North American Water and Power Alliance, which would bring 110 million acre-feet (the average annual natural flow of the Colorado is under 15 million acre-feet) from Northern Canada to the Southwest, the Great Lakes, and the Missouri-Mississippi River systems. The "Christmas tree" that would have to be assembled to put that in the mode of distributive politics boggles the mind. In my judgment, political, economic, and ecological considerations make it unimaginable that any large quantities of outside water will be brought into the Colorado Basin in the foreseeable future. The end of an era appears to be at hand.

The Montana Coal Tax

Compared with the Byzantine happenings in the Colorado Basin, this case seems relatively clear-cut. While seldom put in these terms, the perception of several interested parties is that market and public policy developments have produced a situation in which the exploitation of western coal can generate large economic rents, and this has set off a scramble for their appropriation. One form this has taken in the coal-rich states—especially the most favored ones, Montana and Wyoming—is drastically increased severance taxes.[9] Indeed, the Montana statute actually incorporates the idea of taxing away rent.

In the world of severance taxes, however, taxes on coal still are relatively small. Nationally, oil and natural gas severance taxes account for more than 85 percent of all minerals severance taxes and coal for only about 8 percent. With price deregulation, the percentage attributable to oil and natural gas probably will rise even further.

Nevertheless, the high rates levied on coal in Wyoming and especially Montana have drawn national attention.[10] Not only is the unprecedented level of the Montana tax a controversial issue, but also the fact that most of the coal subject to it is on federal land and used out of state. The result has been court cases and an important Supreme Court decision. Agreement generally exists that states should be permitted to recover indirect costs (roads, schools, and so forth) associated with mining. But there is strong disagreement about how large these costs actually are and about the practice of the states of putting part of the revenues from natural resources taxation in a "trust fund."

The opposing views are well summarized by Rep. Tom Tauke (R-Iowa) and Sen. Max Baucus (D-Montana).[11] Tauke is reported saying:

> These two States (Montana and Wyoming) have attempted to take inordinate advantage of the increases in coal production by imposing excessive severance taxes on the extraction of coal. The taxes—30 percent and 17 percent, respectively—far exceed the costs these two States might incur during the extraction process. As it is now, coal producers pay the costs of reclaiming coal-producing land, and the Federal Government helps subsidize States which incur costs during the development of coal from Federal land. The issue is one of equity.

Senator Baucus has stated:

> I should point out that Montana's citizens voted two to one in 1976 to create this trust fund. They could just as easily have voted for immediate tax relief. But we must recognize that Montana's coal is a nonrenewable resource. Some day it is going to run out. Montanans have long experience with natural resource development. We know that the costs of development do not end when the resources are gone. Fabulous gold deposits and then fabulous copper reserves were exploited—and sent out of State. Today these resources are largely gone. But the environmental and social damages remain—and are still being paid for by Montanans. Montanans also watched the coal boom in Appalachia. We saw what happened when the boom turned to bust—the abject poverty. Mr. President, Montanans believe that we should not come to the Federal Government for help in dealing with the

problems of energy development. So, we have moved to fill that void by imposing a reasonable and responsible tax on coal.

The amounts of money involved are not earth-shaking but, for less-populated states such as Montana, they are significant. Montana's 30 percent levy enacted in 1975 produced $71 million in 1980—nearly double the amount of the previous year. Moreover, and more important, if the tax continues, revenues will rise substantially as development proceeds.

While most of the attention has been on Montana's tax, people from energy-poor states also have expressed broader concerns. In opening hearings on a bill he introduced (more about this later), Sen. David F. Durenberger (IR–Minnesota) said:

> This matter now takes on increased importance in light of President Reagan's efforts to return more responsibility to the states—the philosophy of devolution. As the transfer of income and tax base continues from energy poor to energy rich states, we must carefully consider the increased burden devolution carries with it. Is it feasible to return responsibility to states so widely different in their economic base without a corresponding federal policy designed to compensate for these disparities? Is it fair to expect the states and localities that suffer from a declining economy to provide the same level of public services as those states flush with energy generated revenues? Is it desirable in a federal system to accept the vastly different levels of public services that will inevitably result from an unabated flow of energy dollars?[12]

Seen in this broader context, the Montana tax takes on a larger significance. I turn first to the legal arguments that swirl about the tax.

The Supreme Court Case

Few dispute the right of states to levy severance taxes at some level to recover the costs that mineral development imposes on the state. But in a case appealed to the U.S. Supreme Court (*Commonwealth Edison, et al.* v. *Montana, et al.*, argued March 30, 1981 and decided July 2, 1981) certain Montana coal producers and eleven of their out-of-state utility company customers sought refunds of severance taxes paid under protest and declaratory and injunctive relief, claiming that the tax was invalid under the Commerce and Supremacy Clauses of the United States Constitution. Their claim first was heard in Montana state courts.

The trial court upheld the tax, and the Montana Supreme Court affirmed.

Some background on previous rulings on Commerce Clause claims against severance taxes will be useful before turning to the U.S. Supreme Court's ruling on the present case. In sum, the early decisions established a simple but rather formalistic basis for the tax.[13]

During the 1920s, when *laissez-faire* economics was supported by the judiciary, the Court decided a series of resource tax cases known as the "Heisler Trilogy." Dumars and Brown describe them as follows:

> In each case the particular tax was challenged on Commerce Clause grounds, with the companies asserting that the challenged taxes posed an undue burden on and discriminated against interstate commerce. In each of the three cases the Supreme Court rejected the Commerce Clause contention on the ground that the act of severance precedes the flow of commerce and is therefore not subject to Commerce Clause strictures.
>
> The issue of *Heisler* v. *Thomas Colliery Co.* was framed in terms that virtually track the modern problem. The anthracite coal being taxed in Pennsylvania was found only in a few counties of Pennsylvania and essentially nowhere else, thereby giving the state monopoly powers. Eighty percent of total production was shipped out of state, and the coal was deemed a necessity in the consuming state due to local laws prohibiting the use of other coal for heating. These facts—markedly similar to the present reality of modern western coal and uranium resources—gave rise to the Commerce Clause-based argument that "a tax upon anthracite coal is largely a tribute upon the consumption of other states."
>
> The Court in *Heisler* flatly rejected the Commerce Clause argument, holding that the tax on coal "mined . . . (and) prepared for market" precedes the time at which it is "governed and protected by the national law of commercial regulation." The Court reached that result quite clearly because it could see no limit to the Commerce Clause contention being advanced.
>
> [The Court said]
>
> "If the possibility, or, indeed, certainty of exportation of a product or article from a State determines it to be in interstate commerce before the commencement of its movement from the State, it would seem to follow that it is in such commerce from the instant of its growth or production, and in the case of coals, as they lie in the ground. The result would be curious. It would nationalize all industries, it would nationalize and withdraw from state jurisdiction and deliver to federal

commercial control the fruits of California and the South, the wheat of the West and its meats, the cotton of the South, the shoes of Massachusetts and the woolen industries of other States, at the very inception of their production or growth, that is, the fruits unpicked, the cotton and wheat ungathered, hides and flesh of cattle yet 'on the hoof,' wool yet unshorn, and coal yet unmined, because they are in varying percentages destined for and surely to be exported to States other than those of their production."

After *Heisler* it soon became axiomatic that "mining is not interstate commerce," and that states are free to enact privilege or occupation taxes on the mining or production of resources without violating the Commerce Clause. This early distinction between "local business" preceding commerce and "the flow of interstate commerce" became the legal test that has essentially insulated state resource taxation from successful Commerce Clause challenge up to the present day.

The distinction in *Heisler* between "local business" preceding interstate commerce and the actual interstate flow of commerce protected state resource taxation from successful Commerce Clause challenge until *Commonwealth Edison*. Writing before this case was decided, after reviewing a number of related cases, particularly *Complete Auto Transit, Inc.* v. *Brady*,[14] Dumars and Brown concluded, with considerable foresight, that the formalistic test of *Heisler* no longer would provide a firm defense for severance taxation. In *Complete Auto Transit*, which upheld a Mississippi tax on the "privilege" of doing interstate business, the Court stated that it had "moved toward a standard of permissibility of state taxation based upon its actual effect rather than its legal terminology."

As predicted, the Court in *Commonwealth Edison* said "a state severance tax is not immunized from Commerce Clause scrutiny by a claim that a tax is imposed on goods prior to their entry into the stream of interstate commerce. Any contrary statements in *Heisler* v. *Thomas Colliery Co. 260 U.S. 245* and its progeny are disapproved."

The Court went on to say, also as predicted, that the appropriate tests for the constitutionality of the tax were those set forth in *Complete Auto Transit*. These are that a state tax does not conflict with the Commerce Clause if (1) it is applied to an activity with a substantial nexus with the taxing state; (2) it is fairly apportioned; (3) it does not discriminate against interstate commerce; and (4) it is fairly related to services provided by the state.

The Court ruled that the Montana tax was valid on all counts. Even though 90 percent of Montana's coal is shipped to other states, the Court judged that it did not discriminate against interstate commerce because it was uniformly applied to all coal regardless of destination. The Court further overruled the appellants' claim that the tax was not fairly related to the services provided by the state because "the Montana tax, a general revenue tax, is in proper proportion to appellants' activities within the State and therefore, to their enjoyment of the opportunities and protection which the State has afforded in connection with those activities, such as police and fire protection, the benefit of a trained work force, and the advantages of a civilized society."

The Court also ruled that the tax is not in conflict with the Supremacy Clause because the Minerals Land Leasing Act of 1920 as amended explicitly authorized the states to impose severance taxes on federal lessees without imposing any limits on the amount of such taxes. In addition, it disallowed the argument that the tax violates national energy policies that encourage the use of coal because it judged that congressional intent in passing the legislation was not to preempt all state legislation that may adversely affect the use of coal.

To this layman, the ruling says that there is no legal limit to the size of a severance tax as long as it is fairly related to the activities of the taxed party in a state; presumably the state could extract the entire economic rent of the resource or possibly more if it has any monopoly power. Apparently, a percentage *ad valorem* tax meets this "fairly related" criterion. But the Court also said, "The appropriate level or rate of taxation is essentially a matter for legislative not judicial resolution," thus bouncing the severance tax ball to the Congress. But there was no lack of activity on Capitol Hill about the matter even before the Court ruled.

Congressional Activity

Near universal agreement now exists among interested and affected parties that severance taxation, even on federal lands, is legal; and that states should be able to recover costs associated with mineral extraction activities, and that severance taxes are a suitable means of doing that. As the quotations from Representative Tauke and Senator Baucus illustrate, the argument is really over how high those costs actually are and whether it is legitimate for the state to collect taxes on federal land to compensate the future through trust funds for the depletion of the resource and for any environmental damage that may remain. The trust fund issue is summarized neatly in the Library of Congress document cited earlier.

> The conflict over whether a trust fund (which other States besides Montana and Wyoming have) is a legitimate use of severance taxes is, in part, a conflict over philosophy. Those in favor of trust funds feel that mineral deposits are the natural heritage of all people within a State, and therefore future generations also have an interest in their use. Hence, States are justified in saving some of the compensation from the irretrievable loss of the resource for future generations in the form of a trust fund. Opponents disagree in two ways. First, opponents point to the fact that much of Montana's and Wyoming's coal is under Federal, not State lands, and therefore the natural heritage of the coal is the Federal Government's, not the State's. Second, opponents argue that the only legitimate use of severance taxes is to alleviate adverse impacts from mineral extraction; that the economic benefits from that activity are adequate compensation for the State.[15]

Even before the Supreme Court put the matter squarely in the hands of Congress, bills had been introduced in both the House and the Senate attempting to set limits to taxes and fees on minerals extraction. The stakes appear to be high. Detroit Edison Company, for example, claims that it alone will pay an additional $1 billion for contracted coal over the next twenty years unless state severance taxes are capped.[16]

The scope of proposed legislation varies widely: some bills cover only coal, others include all energy resources, some cover all coal, and others include only coal produced on federal land. But they all agree on one thing: the limit on severance taxes should be 12.5 percent—the percentage traditionally allotted to a state of revenues from oil and gas leases on federal lands within its borders. One bill, however, would permit a higher rate if the state can convincingly show that it is needed.[17] The currently most popular bill (97th Cong., 1 sess., S. 178), sponsored by Senator Durenberger, would place a 12.5 percent cap on state taxes on coal mined on federal lands only. Major energy users vow to lobby strongly for it.[18]

If this bill or one like it passes, Congress will be saying to the states that they may levy severance taxes on coal extracted from the federal lands, and that they may cover—perhaps even generously—any additional concrete and immediate costs imposed on them by the activity. But they will also be told, at least by implication, that they may not extract any additional rent, even for the purpose of setting up trust funds.

Also, if such a law passes, the state might wish to contest it on Tenth Amendment (the "reserved powers" or "states' rights" amendment) grounds, although the Court's ruling in this case would appear to make such a contest unpromising. I turn in the next section to a case that involves the issue of states' rights in a central way.

Uneasy Questions

Before proceeding, however, I want to note some uneasy questions raised by the Court's explicitly and completely handing over the question of how high severance tax rates may be (or should be) to the legislative branch, and the probability of Congress legislating in this area.

The Court's ruling permits states to set rates as high as they wish. On the other hand, if the populous net energy-consuming states could get necessary political support, they could decide that a less-populated state like Montana should have a rate of close to zero, and in the situation the Court created, there could be no legal recourse. None of the proposed legislation has contemplated doing anything like that, but one still may wonder if the Court has not gone too far in simply washing its hands of the whole matter. Furthermore, states and localities tax all sorts of nonresource commodities where a natural or man-made advantage over other similar goods or services creates a tappable rent. New York taxes theater tickets, many areas attractive to tourists have hotel room taxes, and Iowa is seriously proposing to tax corn.[19] Is Congress on the way to regulating state and local taxes on everything that enters interstate commerce? The Durenberger bill limits rates only on coal mined on federal land, but where will it all end?

Finally, the proposed 12.5 percent rate is completely arbitrary, as indeed would be any flat rate proposed to apply across the country. But Montana's 30 percent rate notwithstanding, nearly all severance tax rates are now well below 12.5 percent. Would such a limit become a *target* for state taxation rather than a *ceiling*? Would states regard it as a rate condoned by Congress and relatively immune from legal or political challenge? If that were the case, the regulation would backfire very noisily. For example, if Texas raised its present 4.6 percent severance tax on oil and natural gas to 12.5 percent and there were no significant effect on the demand for the Texas product, 1979 revenues of little over

$1 billion would soar to about $2.5 billion per year. A thorny nest of issues has been uncovered by the Montana tax and subsequent efforts to limit it.

A closing note: late in January of 1982, the Supreme Court decided a case contesting the right of the Jicarilla Apache tribe and other tribes to levy a severance tax on oil and natural gas.[20] The tribe contended that—under various acts of Congress and given its inherent sovereignty under its treaty with the United States—it has the right to levy a severance tax on oil and gas produced on the reservation. The Court ruled in favor of the tribe. Given the amount of energy resources presently and potentially producible on Indian land, this decision makes the overall situation immensely more complex. For example, can both the tribes and the states now tax the same gas? This issue is sure to be tested in court. If they can, and Congress passes severance tax-limiting legislation, will each sovereign party be allowed a limit of 12.5 percent? If not, who will decide what portion each party can take?

The Waste Isolation Pilot Plant Controversy

In 1980, at a place called Gorleben, the West German government set out to drill a test borehole into bedded salt to help determine the suitability of the formation for the storage of nuclear wastes. Before drilling could get under way, a group of several hundred mostly young protesters built a village on the site in the style of an ancient Germanic tribe called the Wends, who once inhabited the area. They declared their village the Republic of Free Wendland and issued Wendish passports to the participants. One of the participants went to Greece and immigration officials routinely stamped his passport, whereupon, in a spirit of jest, the Wendlanders claimed recognition by the Greek government. After three months, a heavily armed military force consisting mostly of border guards (Gorleben is close to the East German border) appeared early one morning and cleared the protesters from the site. The Republic of Free Wendland was bulldozed away. The drilling now proceeds inside what can only be called a fortress, complete with high walls, observation posts, and mounted water cannons.

What to do with nuclear waste—especially high-level and transuranic wastes—is one of the most difficult, contentious, and important issues facing the nuclear nations. *High-level wastes* are products of the reprocessing of commercial reactor fuel and certain military nuclear processes. They are intensely hot, radioactive, and extremely toxic, and some have half-lives ranging to many thousands of years.[21] *Transuranic wastes* are various objects (gloves, protective clothing, tools, and so forth) that have been contaminated by transuranic elements (plutonium, for example). They generally are less radioactive than high-level wastes, but still are very dangerous unless managed carefully.

Nothing on the Gorleben scale has happened in the United States. But in its own way an event that took place in Santa Fe, New Mexico, on May 14, 1981, is almost as extreme. On that day, New Mexico Attorney General Jeff Bingaman filed a complaint in the United States District Court for the District of New Mexico against the Department of Energy (DOE) seeking "declaratory, injunctive, and mandatory relief . . . to protect and vindicate rights guaranteed to the State of New Mexico and its citizens under the United States Constitution and state and federal laws and regulations which have been violated by the defendants in their efforts to construct a nuclear waste repository at the 'Los Medanos' site in Eddy County, New Mexico, approximately 25 miles east of Carlsbad."

What makes this case especially remarkable is that the DOE is, through its contractors, by far the largest employer in the state, at such facilities as the Los Alamos National Laboratory and the Sandia Laboratory. Moreover, the nuclear age started in New Mexico, and its citizens are quite accustomed to having nuclear materials around. What could have happened to induce New Mexico to bite the main hand that feeds it?

Background on WIPP

Although nuclear wastes also come from a number of subsidiary sources, the weapons program—dating from before the end of World War II— and commercial power reactors are by far the largest sources. Some 300,000 cubic meters of high-level waste and nearly 400,000 cubic meters of transuranic wastes now exist, all in some form of temporary storage or buried in trenches, the latter mostly at the DOE's Hanford, Washington, and Savannah River, South Carolina, laboratories. And each year the figures grow.

Since the middle 1950s, most scientists schooled in the matter have seen salt deposits as a promising location for permanent nuclear waste repositories. The presence of the salt itself indicates a lack of liquid water for millions of years, and the plasticity of the salt is regarded as an advantage. Experiments were done by the Atomic Energy Commission (AEC, whose functions are now embodied in DOE) during the middle 1960s in a salt mine near Lyons, Kansas, and in 1970 the AEC selected the Lyons site as the chief contender for the location of a nuclear waste repository. But the Kansas state geologist opposed the Lyons site because of concern that the many holes drilled into the formation at various times might be a path for water to flow into the repository at some future date. Under this state opposition, the AEC abandoned plans for the Lyons site.

In the early 1970s the AEC investigated sites in southeastern New Mexico, and field tests were begun there. The intent was to test the site as a possible repository for *commercial wastes,* which occur when spent fuel rods of reactors are reprocessed to remove most of their plutonium (which can be used as reactor fuel). Later, the Carter administration, citing the dangers associated with having large amounts of plutonium around (among other things, it is prime bomb material), decided not to go forward with commercial reprocessing, and there still is no clear indication of whether spent fuel rods ever will be reprocessed. The economics of reprocessing also are questionable.

Thus, in a sense there is no commercial high-level waste. The spent fuel rods are in holding pools at the reactor sites awaiting a decision about whether they ultimately will be reprocessed or must themselves be regarded as dangerous wastes to be disposed of. However, commercial activities have produced a substantial amount of transuranic waste, and a great deal more will be added to the total if and when Three Mile Island is cleaned up.

Interest eventually shifted back to mined repositories for both military high-level and transuranic wastes and civilian wastes. In 1975 Sandia Laboratories in Albuquerque, New Mexico, was funded to again investigate salt formations in southeastern New Mexico.

After a false start at another site, which proved to be questionable, the Los Medanos site was selected for what has come to be called the Waste Isolation Pilot Plant (WIPP). In late 1977 WIPP was authorized by Congress for research and development purposes with respect to *military transuranic wastes.* Then came a series of fits and starts as DOE and its clients in Congress changed and rechanged their minds about the nature and scope of WIPP. Shortly after the congressional authorization, still in 1977, the Department of Energy (DOE had now been established to replace the Energy Research and Development Administration) told the Nuclear Regulatory Commission (NRC) that the scope of WIPP would be expanded to include *military high-level wastes*. Inclusion of them would have required licensing by NRC, a thorough but time-consuming procedure. In the spring of 1978, a DOE task force urged that WIPP be a demonstration project for disposal of *commercial high-level wastes*. Finally, in late 1979, the fitful planning came full circle: Congress authorized WIPP as a research and development facility for military transuranic wastes exempt from NRC licensing, and late in 1980 Congress authorized a total of $199 million to proceed with the project.

The State's Complaint

What happened along the way to cause New Mexico to sue the Department of Energy to get injunctive relief? Importantly, the state never has opposed, in principle, the establishment of a nuclear waste repository within its boundaries. But New Mexico nevertheless understandably became confused by DOE's constantly redefining the scope of the project, a confusion that evolved into a certain mistrust. The state also was frustrated by DOE's failure to involve it in decision making that would assure an effective state role in assessing the safety of the project. Moreover, the state felt left out of the decision process when it came to securing help in meeting major offsite costs the state otherwise would have to bear, including road construction and repair, security forces, and emergency response capabilities.

More specifically, the sequence of the most pertinent events was as follows:[22]

- 1978-79: High-level DOE officials promised New Mexico officials state concurrence and NRC licensing of WIPP. State officials relied on those promises in agreeing that the Los Medanos site should be examined as a possible waste repository.
- Mid-1979: To satisfy the wishes of the House Armed Services Committee and to conserve funding for WIPP, DOE agreed that it would not seek licensing for the project and that it would not follow through on its promise to give New Mexico concurrence rights. An opinion rendered at the time by the General Accounting Office concluded that a prior agreement between DOE and Louisiana providing for state concurrence was not legally binding and that it merely con-

stituted a code of behavior that could be breached unilaterally. This made New Mexico wary that any agreement it did make would be legally binding.

- December 1979: Congress passed Public Law 996-164, authorizing WIPP to proceed, including sinking of an exploratory shaft. The law also directs the secretary of energy to seek to reach a "consultation and cooperation" agreement with the state no later than September 30, 1980, which would establish procedures for the resolution of state concerns.

- 1980: Negotiations proceeded between DOE and a special state task force appointed by the governor in an effort to reach the legally required agreement. A draft agreement was reached, but the attorney general's office found a number of legal deficiencies in it. The primary objection was that DOE would not agree to a legally binding document that would provide for judicial review of agency actions. In September, during negotiations with the task force to try to resolve the legal issues, the attorney general's office reported that the DOE's chief negotiator stated that DOE had no legal obligation to reach an agreement prior to proceeding with the WIPP and that, in his opinion, DOE did not need any agreement.

- January 1981: DOE announced its publication of the WIPP Record of Decision which authorized it to proceed with phased construction and operation of the WIPP. That decision was made without any prior state consultation.

New Mexico's complaint came on May 14, 1981. In an opening paragraph, the state's case is put succinctly:

The course of conduct pursued by the defendant DOE and the other defendants named herein in seeking to construct the WIPP project in New Mexico has unconstitutionally intruded upon the sovereignty of the State of New Mexico in important and traditional areas of state governmental functions and responsibilities. The defendants' conduct has also violated state and federal laws by (a) failing to obtain the State's concurrence before commencement of WIPP construction activities; (b) refusing to sign an enforceable agreement with the State resolving the State's many legitimate concerns with the project in a timely manner; (c) failing to comply with the National Environmental Policy Act of 1969 ("NEPA") in the preparation of an adequate environmental impact statement for the project; (d) and failing to comply with the Federal Land Policy and Management Act of 1976

("FLPMA") in the segregation and withdrawal of public land at the Los Medanos site for the project.

A few days before the hearing on the complaint, scheduled to start July 8, 1981, DOE capitulated on the main points blocking the agreement. The state attorney general then was able to issue the following statement:

> The State of New Mexico today has obtained a federal court order providing the State a meaningful role in the decision making process of the Waste Isolation Pilot Plant (WIPP) Project. The order, issued by U.S. District Judge Juan Burciaga, requires compliance with a contract that preserves the State's right to protect the health and welfare of its citizens, and imposes on the federal departments of Energy and Interior and the Bureau of Land Management several significant requirements that must be met before the WIPP Project can proceed.
>
> As I stated when the State filed its WIPP suit May 14, it is not New Mexico's intention to block the placement of an underground radioactive waste repository in the State. It is our intention to assert New Mexico's statutory and constitutional right to protect our citizens by our active participation in the crucial decisions of such a project. Through this court order, we have made major progress toward that goal. The order in no way prejudices the claims we are making in that suit.
>
> The order includes the consultation and cooperation agreement negotiated by State and DOE officials last year, with the provision that the agreement is enforceable in the courts and does not waive any rights the State has to judicial review of federal actions. Those two essential elements—judicial review and enforceability—blocked the signing of the agreement by DOE last September. Since our suit was filed, however, the federal government has shifted its position to accommodate the State on those issues.
>
> Now, for the first time, New Mexico has a binding and enforceable legal mechanism for asserting its rights to be actively involved in this critical undertaking.[23]

As the earlier quotation from the Complaint indicates, the state's case rested on three general arguments—that its Tenth Amendment constitutional rights were being violated, that DOE violated NEPA (environmental impact statement) requirements, and that the Department of the Interior illegally withdrew (that is, closed to multiple use) federal lands for WIPP. The total impact of these arguments apparently was sufficiently compelling to cause DOE not to want to go to a trial on the merits of the state's case.

Of the three, I believe the second and the third were the more telling, because straightforward states' rights arguments for many years have met with very little success in the federal courts. Nevertheless, this line of argument is interesting in light of the recent strongly renewed political attention to states' rights and the possibility that Tenth Amendment claims may be made more frequently in the future. After reviewing briefly the NEPA and land withdrawal arguments, I will go into the states' rights arguments in a little more detail.

The essence of the NEPA violation claim is as follows. First, there is an inadequate analysis of alternatives. For example, the alternative of storage in geological structures other than salt is given scant attention and the no-action alternative (required by NEPA) is dismissed in a few sentences. The latter is particularly striking since the Environmental Impact Statement itself says that the particular transuranic wastes DOE says it will put in the repository, if it proves feasible, can be left safely where they are (in Idaho) "for at least a hundred years." Second, between the time of the Draft Environmental Impact Statement and the Final Environmental Impact Statement, an entirely new type of approach to testing the geological feasibility of the site was introduced, called the Site and Preliminary Design Validation Program. This program is designed so that the test structures ultimately could become part of the repository itself. The state contends that this in itself constitutes a major federal action that is required to go through the environmental impact statement process and that therefore the alleged final statement, for the first time explaining the project, is actually a draft statement and cannot legally support the Record of Decision.

On the land withdrawal issue, New Mexico claims that the actions of the defendants, the Departments of Energy and the Interior and the Bureau of Land Management, in withdrawing land for the project proceeded in an illegal manner. The land never was officially withdrawn by the Bureau of Land Management (in the sense that a public statement to that effect was issued), but it was held segregated for WIPP use from December 1978 to the time the Complaint was filed. The state claims this is *de facto* withdrawal and therefore violates FLPMA by the defendant's failure to report the withdrawal to Congress and to hold public hearings in New Mexico, both of which are required by the act. Other claims of wrongful and illegal actions were made in the Complaint. One which was not included there but might have figured importantly in the trial, had it occurred, could have been made under the Tenth Amendment to the U.S. Constitution.

The Tenth Amendment Claim

As previously noted, states' rights arguments citing the Tenth Amendment have not fared well in the federal courts in modern times. The one recent case consistently cited by constitutional lawyers as lending some support for Tenth Amendment arguments is a 1976 case, *National League of Cities* v. *Usery*.[24] The Supreme Court was sharply divided in this case, but it held that Congress lacked the power under the Commerce Clause to prescribe minimum wages and maximum hours for state employees under the Fair Labor Standards Act. Its holding is founded on constitutional policy reflected in the Tenth Amendment that "there are limits upon the power of Congress to override state sovereignty. . . ." The Court held that in attempting to exercise its commerce power to prescribe wages and hours for state employees, the Congress had—and the language here is very important for present purposes—"sought to wield its power in a fashion that would impair the states' ability to function effectively in a federal system."

One might reasonably expect that a project like WIPP, with its national defense relationship, would be the very worst case for making states' rights arguments. For some rather special reasons, however, this might not be so. To see why, it is useful to quote fairly extensively from the legislation authorizing WIPP.[25]

> Sec. 213(a) The Secretary of Energy shall proceed with the Waste Isolation Pilot Plant construction project authorized to be carried out in the Delaware Basin of southeast New Mexico (project 77-13-f) in accordance with the authorization for such project as modified by this section. Notwithstanding any other provision of law, the Waste Isolation Pilot Plant is authorized as a defense activity of the Department of Energy, administered by the Assistant Secretary of Energy for Defense Programs, for the express purpose of providing a research and development facility to demonstrate the safe disposal of radioactive wastes resulting from the defense activities and programs of the United States exempted from regulation by the Nuclear Regulatory Commission.
>
> (b)(1) In carrying out such project, the Secretary shall consult and cooperate with the appropriate officials of the State of New Mexico, with respect to the public health and safety concerns of such State in

regard to such project and shall, consistent with the purposes of sub-section (a), give consideration to such concerns and cooperate with such officials in resolving such concerns. The consultation and coop-eration required by this paragraph shall be carried out as provided in paragraph (2).

(2) The Secretary shall seek to enter into a written agreement with the appropriate officials of the State of New Mexico, as provided by the laws of the State of New Mexico, not later than September 30, 1980, setting forth the procedures under which the consultation and cooperation required by paragraph (1) shall be carried out. Such pro-cedures shall include as a minimum—

(A) the right of the State of New Mexico to comment on, and make recommendations with regard to, the public health and safety aspects of such project before the occurrence of certain key events identified in the agreement;

(B) procedures, including specific time frames, for the Secretary to receive, consider, resolve, and act upon comments and recommendations made by the State of New Mexico; and

(C) procedures for the Secretary and the appropriate officials of the State of New Mexico to periodically review, amend, or modify the agreement.

This quotation contains two items of special note. First, Congress wanted to make absolutely certain that everyone understood that WIPP was a defense activity, presumably to assure that NRC licensing would not be necessary. Second, while there is some ambiguity in the language, it appears to be the clear intent of Congress that a workable effective agreement be struck with New Mexico before work on WIPP began.

While a national defense argument might have short-circuited any attempt to invoke the Tenth Amendment, it seems doubtful that DOE would have chosen to use it. The reason is that a 1958 federal law (43 U.S. Code Sec. 155) states that only Congress can withdraw land for defense purposes. It would be hard to argue that WIPP should not be regarded as a defense activity since Congress went to such pains to say that it is. If WIPP then were held to be subject to the above-cited federal law, the whole enterprise would sink, at least for a time.

The other key to why Tenth Amendment arguments might have re-ceived a favorable hearing in this case also is found in WIPP's authorizing legislation. DOE's failure to negotiate an effective workable agreement with New Mexico prior to starting work on WIPP clearly was contrary to the intent of Congress. On this basis, New Mexico would have argued that DOE was violating its constitutional right to protect the health and welfare of its citizens, a right that Congress had recognized explicitly in the statute and, in the language of *League of Cities*, that would have impaired its ability "to function effectively in a federal system."

If the courts finally had ruled that the Tenth Amendment claims were valid, as seems distinctly possible because of the special circumstances surrounding the case, it would not have been the basis for a general assertion of states' rights around the country, because of those special circumstances. But the case is interesting because it comes at the beginning of an era in which the Supreme Court may be more apt to listen sympathetically to states' rights arguments. Furthermore, it is an unusual, if not unique, instance in which a particular state is, if not an equal, then at least an important partner with the federal government in a project widely regarded as of critical national importance.

Postscript

Under the agreement with DOE, New Mexico specified certain further scientific tests to verify the safety of the WIPP site. Specifically, they were intended to shed additional light on a "disturbed zone" in an area located north of the center of the WIPP site, an area where anomalous seismic reflections made it impossible to characterize the geology from the surface. During drilling into this zone on November 22, 1981, a highly pressurized brine reservoir was encountered only about 560 feet horizontally distant from the proposed location of the nuclear waste storage area and 790 feet below it. This means there is a potential for movement into the repository and later transport of wastes to the biosphere. This unexpected finding therefore has cast doubt upon the entire suitability of the storage site. As of February 1982, tests are being performed to evaluate the volume, geometric boundaries, origin, age, and possible interconnections with other reservoirs.[26]

Notes

1. For an excellent detailed discussion of all aspects of the issue, the reader may wish to consult the January 1975 issue of the *Natural Resources Journal*.

2. *Department of State Bulletin* vol. 69 (September 24, 1973) p. 391.

3. Dean Mann, "Politics and the Salinity Problem," *Natural Resources Journal* vol. 15 (January 1975).

4. Ibid., pp. 127-128.

5. John V. Krutilla, "The International Columbia River Treaty: An Economic Evaluation," in Allen V. Kneese and Stephen C. Smith, eds., *Water Research* (Baltimore, Md., Johns Hopkins University Press for Resources for the Future, 1966) p. 96. See also, John V. Krutilla, *The Columbia River Treaty: The Economics of an International River Basin Development* (Baltimore, Md., Johns Hopkins University Press for Resources for the Future, 1967).

6. Actually, such larger factors seem to have been important in all the major Mexican–American water agreements. During the 1939–44 negotiations over the Colorado and the Rio Grande, in which the United States agreed to an allocation of 1.5 million acre-feet per year of Colorado River water to Mexico, an amount far above historical use in the Mexicali Valley, the United States clearly wished to cultivate friendly relations with other countries, especially neighboring ones, during World War II. In that case, however, the situation was more complex than the present one since agreements for both rivers were being negotiated simultaneously, and the United States did have a direct economic interest in reaching an agreement on the Rio Grande. This was so since most of the water in the lower Rio Grande (below Fort Quitman, Texas) originates from Mexican tributaries. For this reason, the Mexicans insisted on negotiating about both rivers at the same time.

7. Irving Fox, H. Gotzman, S. Smith, and U. Torti, "Administration of International Rivers," paper presented at the United Nations Panel of Experts on Legal and Institutional Implications of International Water Resources Development, Vienna, Austria, December 9–14, 1968.

8. The extreme and, it seems to me, rather convoluted position of the basin states on not losing water to Mexico is exemplified by the assertion that the U.S. taxpayer should be responsible for replacing the 43,000 acre-feet of brine that will flow from the desalting plant directly to the Gulf of California because, it is argued, this involves an increase in water deliveries to Mexico. See M. Hulbert, "Values and Choices in the Development of an Arid Land Base," paper presented before a meeting of the American Association for the Advancement of Science, San Francisco, California, February 24–March 1, 1974.

9. For a discussion of efforts to appropriate rents, see Albert Church, *Conflicts Over Resource Ownership: The Use of Public Policy by Private Interests* (Lexington, Mass., Lexington Books, 1982).

10. The coal taxes are on an *ad valorem* basis; some people in the region prefer to compute them on a Btu basis, which makes them look more comparable with existing taxes on oil and natural gas.

11. Both quotations are from Larry Parker, *Energy: Limiting State Coal Severance Taxes*, Issue Brief No. 1B80060 (Washington, D.C., Library of Congress, Congressional Research Service, November 1980).

12. Opening Statement by Sen. David Durenberger (IR–Minn.), Subcommittee on

Intergovernmental Relations, Fiscal Disparities Hearing on the Commerce Clause and Severance Taxes, July 15 and 16, 1981.

13. A thorough analysis of the background is found in Charles Dumars and F. Lee Brown, *Legal Issues in State Taxation of Energy Development*, NMEI Report No. 77-1121 (Albuquerque, New Mexico Energy Institute at the University of New Mexico, November 1979).

14. 430 U.S. 274 (1977).

15. Parker, *Energy*.

16. *Business Week* (July 27, 1981) p. 94.

17. The question of what the real costs are can be very contentious. In the case of Montana, the costs calculated by the state are *thirty-five times* higher than those calculated by a consultant for several midwestern utilities (see Prepared Statement by Sally Hunt Streiter, *Hearings on the Commerce Clause and Severance Taxes*, submitted to the Subcommittee on Intergovernmental Relations, Committee on Governmental Affairs, United States Senate, Washington, D.C., July 15, 1981).

18. *Business Week*, p. 94.

19. "A New Civil War Looms Over State Taxes on Natural Resources," *The Washington Post*, August 19, 1981, p. A8.

20. The argument for the tribes can be found in Nos. 80-11 and 80-15 in The Supreme Court of the United States, October Term, 1980, Brief for the Respondent Jicarilla Apache Tribe.

21. A half-life is the time required for half the atoms of a radioactive substance present to disintegrate. For example, the half-life of plutonium 239, a common element in reactor fuel wastes, is more than 24,000 years.

22. Adapted from an unpublished internal memorandum from the New Mexico State Attorney General's Office.

23. Attorney General Jeff Bingaman's Statement on WIPP Court Order, Santa Fe, New Mexico, photocopy.

24. A discussion can be found in Testimony of Walter Hellerstein before the Subcommittee on Intergovernmental Relations of the U.S. Senate Committee on Governmental Affairs, "Fiscal Disparities, Part II: The Commerce Clause and State Severance Taxes," July 15, 1981.

25. Laws of the 96th Cong., 1 sess., 93 Stat. 1266.

26. Information from In the United States District Court for the State of New Mexico, *Report of the Plaintiff, State of New Mexico, on The Status of the WIPP Litigation* (no date).

chapter five

The Legal Structure of
Interstate Resource Conflicts

Richard B. Stewart

We have explored the history of U.S. regional conflict and looked at a
few of its modern manifestations through the prism of the energy "crisis"
that began in 1973–74. In the last chapter three case studies of current
conflicts were examined in some detail. The cases of Colorado River
salinity, the Montana coal tax, and the Waste Isolation Pilot Plant in
New Mexico display important differences, but one striking similarity
is that all three conflicts encountered the legal process at some point,
whether through Indian and international treaties or in the courts, up
to and including the U.S. Supreme Court. As such conflicts typically
engage the legal process, this chapter examines the legal structure for
dealing with regional resource conflicts between and among states and
their political subdivisions (regions as such have no legal standing).

 In the past, the federal courts have taken the initiative in deciding
controversies between states and in invalidating state regulation and
taxation that restrict the free flow of capital and labor through the
national economy. Litigants are demanding that the federal courts play
a similar role in resolving interstate resource conflicts. During its 1980
term, the U.S. Supreme Court heard no fewer than four cases involving

such controversies. In disposing of these cases, however, the Court made clear that the federal judiciary will *not* play a major role in resolving conflicts among states over natural resources. Unless Congress intervenes, states will have considerable freedom to make independent decisions about the development and taxation of resources within their borders.

Political questions in the United States almost inevitably evolve into legal questions, but the courts may decide to remit conflicts for resolution by political and economic processes. In the context of interstate resource conflicts, this judicial retreat is desirable in many respects. For example, as we will see, state taxation and regulation of natural resources that do not by their terms discriminate against other states should be substantially immune from federal judicial scrutiny.

But there is an important class of cases—those involving out-of-state impacts that are not economic—that calls out for a strong federal judicial role. Transboundary pollution is an important example. In most cases, informal bargaining among states cannot resolve conflicts such as that concerning acid rain, or river salinity, in part because of the large number of states involved and because upwind or upstream states have little incentive to bargain, absent offers of "bribes" or side payments from downwind or downstream states. In theory, Congress has ample authority to resolve such conflicts through legislation, but in practice substantial constitutional and political barriers bar effective legislative solutions. The federal judicial retreat in this area has created a vacuum that must be met by new decision-making mechanisms.

The operation of the U.S. federal system historically has been a dialectical process, with alternating surges of centralization and decentralization playing back on one another. The country now is undergoing a surge of decentralization that in my opinion is largely healthy. But the choice is not a simple, sweeping election between state and federal authority. The role of different branches of government—legislative, judicial, and administrative—must be considered, along with the particular problem at issue. Traditional mechanisms of accommodation and resolution have been overstressed by some of the conflicts generated by increased energy and raw material prices, the resulting pressures to develop the sparsely populated and scenic West, environmental insults imposed by modern technologies, and heightened public concern about environmental degradation. The system is far from radical failure, but the adequacy of our institutions to deal with such conflicts clearly must be reexamined.

Framing the Constitution

Conflicts among the states under the Articles of Confederation were a major reason for the adoption in 1789 of a new form of government. There were two basic forms of conflict, and the Constitution contains two principal provisions to deal with them.

One set of conflicts concerned trade and commerce. The Articles denied the national government unitary powers over foreign trade and commerce among the states, and the Confederation consequently suffered in foreign trade dealings. In addition, critics asserted that the system of confederation thwarted internal trade by allowing strategically located port states such as New York to impose tariffs whose incidence fell on consumers in neighboring states, and by failing to deal with state trade barriers designed to protect local industry, including retaliatory tariffs that stifled commerce among the states.[1]

These concerns played a substantial role in the calling of the constitutional convention.[2] Article I of the Constitution sought to deal with them by authorizing Congress "To regulate Commerce with foreign Nations, among the several States. . . ." This power, in the words of *The Federalist,* was seen as necessary to suppress "interfering and unneighborly relations (of states)" that would be "serious sources of animosity and discord . . . if not restrained by national control."[3]

The framers apparently expected that Congress would adopt legislation to promote internal trade and protect it against parochial state regulation and taxation. In the event, however, it was federal judges who assumed the leading role in preventing economic balkanization and helping assure that the United States became one great free trade area.

The threat of armed or other conflict over state borders was a second engine of discord under the Articles of Confederation. Urging the delegates to reach agreement, Elbridge Gerry asserted that, wanting a system of union, "We should be without an Umpire to decide controversies and must be at the mercy of events."[4] The response was the creation of a national tribunal to act as umpire: Article III of the Constitution provides for original jurisdiction by the U.S. Supreme Court over controversies between states. Although its immediate occasion was border disputes and, to a lesser extent, controversies arising out of fraudulent or corrupt conveyances of land by state legislatures, the framers envisaged a broader utility in the power conveyed. As Hamilton asserted in *The Federalist:*

> But there are other sources, besides interfering claims of boundary, from which bickering and animosities may spring up among the members of the union . . . .(I)t is warrantable to apprehend, that the spirit which produced (the border controversies) will assume new shapes that could not be foreseen, nor specifically be provided against. Whatever practices may have a tendency to disturb the harmony of the states are proper objects of federal superintendence and control.[5]

Two other provisions in the Constitution bear on interstate conflicts. Section 10 of Article I provides that no state shall without the consent of Congress enter into any agreement or compact with another state. This provision has been read to authorize states, with the consent of Congress, to enter into legally binding compacts with one another; the terms of the compacts are judicially enforceable as federal law. In cases where states have incentives to negotiate, the Compact Clause provides a mechanism for agreement that federal courts will enforce.[6] In addition, the provision in Article IV, Section 2, that the "Citizens of each State shall be entitled to all Privileges and Immunities of Citizens in the several States" has been invoked by federal courts to invalidate a state's effort to restrict to its own citizens exploitation of natural resources within the state.[7] But inasmuch as the commerce power and the Supreme Court's power to resolve controversies among states have played the largest role in resolving such controversies,[8] the balance of this chapter focuses on the historical development and present state of these powers.

Origins of Commerce Power

The politics of the nineteenth century dictated that regulation and taxation of commerce were largely the task of state and local governments, and consequently Congress did not assert its legislative power to regulate commerce. Motivated by parochial incentives, the state and local governments often imposed restrictions or burdens on interstate commerce in an effort to favor local producers, consumers, or taxpayers. For example, in order to favor local businesses, states sought to prohibit or hinder sales within the state by out-of-state business; to favor local taxpayers, states sought to levy a disproportionately heavy tax burden on interstate enterprise. Up to the early twentieth century, most such efforts by states involved regulation or taxation of retail commerce, of transportation, or of manufacturing industry.

Judicial Initiative

In response, the federal courts during the nineteenth century began to invoke the Commerce Clause to invalidate such restrictive state measures, even in the absence of relevant congressional legislation. Given that the commerce power in Article I is a grant of authority to the Congress, not the courts, this was a remarkable innovation—even, if you will, a usurpation. The stated and rather questionable rationale for the courts' initiative was that congressional silence must be "deemed" a decree that interstate commerce should be free and unregulated.[9] The practical ground for this judicial initiative was the perceived need for some sort of federal intervention to limit parochial state taxation and regulation.

The structure of the problem makes it ill-suited for congressional action. Because most state measures burdening interstate commerce arguably promote some legitimate state interest, the impact of and justification for such measures generally must be examined on a "retail" case-by-case basis. Congress legislates on a wholesale basis: it has neither the resources nor the decision-making structure to review thousands of state and local measures. This is a job for which the courts are better suited.

Some early court decisions rested on the premise that interstate commerce was totally immune from state control. But the steady expansion of interstate commerce in legal definition and economic fact put a growing strain on that position. Indeed, all interstate commerce consists of activities within states. The legitimate interests of a state in taxing and controlling aspects of interstate commerce carried on within it were recognized.

The federal judiciary developed a variety of doctrinal devices to mediate between the competing state and national interests. For example, regulation of "commerce" was distinguished from "local police" regulations. Prohibited "direct" effects on interstate commerce were distinguished from permitted "indirect" effects. In recent decades, more frankly pragmatic approaches have emerged: states may regulate interstate commerce that has a substantial connection with the state provided that, first, the regulation does not discriminate against interstate commerce and, second, the burdens imposed are not excessive in relation to the state interests promoted by the measure. A similar approach prevails with respect to taxation, with special attention given to the danger of duplicative taxation of interstate commerce by several states.[10]

Federal courts—and state courts applying the federal law developed by federal judges—have invalidated hundreds of state measures hindering or burdening retail commerce, transportation, and industry. Consequently, the federal courts' initiatives under the Commerce Clause have played a substantial role in developing a market economy in which resources and commodities move freely from state to state and region to region. The premises of the courts' efforts were most forcefully summed up by Justice Jackson:

> Our system, fostered by the Commerce Clause, is that every farmer and every craftsman shall be encouraged to produce by the certainty that he will have free access to every market in the Nation, that no home embargoes will withhold his exports, and no foreign state will by customs duties or regulation exclude them. Likewise, every consumer may look to the free competition from every producing area in the Nation to protect him from exploitation by any. Such was the vision of the Founders; such has been the doctrine of this Court which has given it reality.[11]

Regulation and Taxation of Natural Resources

How have the federal courts dealt, under the Commerce Clause, with state regulation and taxation of natural resources? As noted, disputes over natural resources only recently have become a major staple of Commerce Clause legislation.[12] In dealing with them, the courts have made some important departures from past approaches developed in the context of retail trade, transportation, and industry.

Market and Nonmarket Impacts

At the outset, one must distinguish state decisions that affect residents of other states through market mechanisms from those with nonmarket impacts. State imposition of environmental controls or severance taxes on in-state coal mining have market impacts, for example, in that they may affect consumers of energy in other states by raising its price. An example of nonmarket impacts is a state decision to permit within its borders the combustion of coal without environmental controls, thus generating air pollution that drifts into a neighboring state. In their Commerce Clause decisions, the courts have been concerned with state decisions that affect commerce in the marketplace. Nonmarket impacts have not been dealt with under the Commerce Clause but, as developed below, under the Court's Article III powers to adjudicate controversies among states.

A state's decision to develop its natural resources has market impacts in other states, as capital and labor flow to the developing state. Some of these impacts may be negative. For example, states from which growth is shifted may lose jobs and tax revenues. But state development decisions that attract growth from other states never have been invalidated by courts under the Commerce Clause. Indeed, the whole object of judicial intervention has been to further such movements in the expectation that they on balance would advance the economic welfare of the nation as a whole.

In contrast, state decisions to impose taxes or regulatory controls on the development and use of natural resources can diminish the free flow of commerce among states or exploit tarifflike powers, and these steps have been the object of judicial concern. As previously noted, the courts developed a two-pronged strategy for dealing with state burdens on commerce, invalidating measures that either discriminate against commerce or impose undue burdens upon it.

State Discrimination

One of the 1980 term's four interstate conflict decisions, *Maryland* v. *Louisiana*,[13] reaffirmed, in the natural resource context, the requirement that a state not discriminate in favor of its own consumers, businesses, or taxpayers. In this case, Louisiana imposed a "first use" tax on gas taken from the Outer Continental Shelf and first brought to shore in Louisiana. Various exemptions or credits were extended to Louisiana consumers, but the tax applied with full force to gas shipped out of the state for consumption elsewhere, and the Court unanimously struck it down as a discriminatory burden on interstate commerce.[14]

In earlier cases, the Supreme Court had made clear that, under the nondiscrimination requirement, states may not prohibit the export of such natural resources as game, natural gas, or groundwater.[15] And the Court recently struck down New Jersey's ban on disposal of out-of-state wastes within its borders, thus extending the nondiscrimination requirement to the use of environmental natural resources—land, water, air— for waste disposal.[16]

Nondiscriminatory Burdens

These decisions all involved measures that explicitly treated in-state citizens or enterprises more advantageously than their out-of-state counterparts. But even a formally nondiscriminatory tax or regulation may impose heavy burdens on interstate commerce. If the goods and services produced by the activity subject to tax or regulation are destined primarily for out-of-state consumers, a state may shift most of the economic burdens of taxation or regulation out of state while retaining most of the benefits. In this situation, the courts traditionally examined the challenged measure to determine whether it was justified by legitimate state interests and whether the burdens imposed on interstate enterprise were reasonable in relation to the legitimate local benefit and the benefits provided by the state to the interstate enterprise.[17] However, in two of the cases decided during the 1980 term, the Supreme Court made clear that it will not review the balance between legitimate local benefits and interstate burdens where a state is engaged in regulation or taxation of natural resources, as opposed to retail trade, transportation, or industrial enterprise generally.

One of these cases, *Commonwealth Edison* v. *Montana*,[18] was discussed in some detail in chapter 4. Recall that eastern energy consumers challenged Montana's severance tax on coal extraction (equal to 30 percent of the coal's value) when roughly 90 percent of the coal was shipped out of state. Although the tax formally was nondiscriminatory— it applied equally to coal consumed within and without the state—purchasers of the exported coal challenged the tax as a monopolistic imposition that far exceeded what Montana reasonably could ask the coal mining industry to contribute to the state's revenues. As noted, the Court sustained the tax without further inquiry (three dissenting justices—concerned that resource-rich states would exploit other states— would require a trial on the reasonableness of the tax). The majority

emphasized the inability of the courts to determine the ultimate incidence of tax measures or the policy question of how states should go
about allocating the burdens of taxation.[19]

The second case, *Minnesota* v. *Cloverleaf Dairy,*[20] involved a challenge
to a Minnesota statute banning the use of nonrecyclable plastic milk
containers while permitting the continued use of paperboard containers
that also could not be recycled. The environmental benefits of such a
ban were sharply disputed; indeed, the lower state court had held that
the real purpose of the measure was to protect the local paper-container
industry against competition from out-of-state manufacturers of plastic
containers. Nevertheless, the Supreme Court's attitude here was even
more deferential than in the Montana case: it concluded that the Minnesota legislature might reasonably find that there were appreciable
environmental benefits from the ban, and that this was enough to out-
weigh whatever burdens on interstate commerce were thereby created.
The Court justified its deference by emphasizing the inability of judges
to assess and resolve conflicting scientific evidence concerning environmental effects, and to weigh environmental benefits against burdens on
commerce.

In these two decisions, the Supreme Court effectively has abandoned,
in the natural resource area, the traditional judicial practice of reviewing
and invalidating state measures that unduly burden commerce, even
though they are not discriminatory. As long as a state takes care to
adopt measures that do not discriminate on their face against out-of-
state citizens or enterprises, the Supreme Court apparently will not
invalidate the measure as an unconstitutional burden on commerce. As
far as the Commerce Clause goes, states may prohibit, severely restrict,
or heavily tax the development of energy resources within their borders.
And they may also restrict or ban the use of their natural resources for
other purposes. For example, they may limit or prohibit the disposal of
radioactive or toxic wastes within their borders.

Explaining Judicial Deference

What explains or justifies the Court's refusal to apply undue-burden-
on-commerce analysis to natural resource measures? Three factors distinguish such measures from state taxation or regulation of trade or
industry generally: the technical complexity of the issues presented; the

systemic regional character of interstate resource conflicts; and the non-market values at stake.

Technical Complexity

Several Supreme Court decisions have noted the limited competence of judges to assess resource regulation and taxation. How can a court determine the environmental benefits of a strip mine regulation, for example, or of a ban on plastic milk bottles, much less begin to weigh those benefits against concommitant burdens on commerce? The limits of the adversary process of forensic proof and of generalist judges in dealing with such matters are apparent.[21]

Assessing the economic consequences of a tax on resource development also involves exquisitely complex and difficult analytical and factual issues.[22] If Montana enjoys near-total market power with respect to the supply of low-sulfur coal, its severance tax would represent a monopolistic imposition. But how does a court determine how much market power Montana enjoys, given the various substitutes for Montana's coal? Moreover, the severance tax may simply represent a successful effort to capture economic rents from producers or the railroads and result in no significant price increases to consumers.

Such issues present acute difficulties for courts, difficulties that probably are greater in the area of natural resource taxation and regulation than in the traditional context of retail trade, transportation, and manufacturing. Still, such obstacles have not discouraged the courts in other areas when they have determined to play a role.[23]

Systemic Regional Character

Nearly all states have attempted to restrict or tax interstate retail commerce, transportation, and manufacturing in an effort to prefer some in-state interest. Every state has had opportunities to do so, and no state or group of states has a dominant position. Courts policing burdens on interstate commerce would blow the whistle now on one state, now on another. But in the natural resource area, a relatively few states—those in the Rocky Mountain area, those along the Gulf Coast, California, and Alaska—do have a dominant position.[24] If the courts were to play an active role in this context, they constantly would be invalidating the measures of one group of states for the benefit of consumers in another group. Judges may well be reluctant to interpose themselves in such a systemic regional conflict, believing that it raises far-reaching distributional issues that must be resolved through means other than adjudication. I am inclined to agree and give this point greater explanatory weight than technical complexity.

Nonmarket Values

The third reason for judicial refusal rigorously to scrutinize natural resource measures by states is the nonmarket character of the values at stake. Regulation and taxation of retail trade, transportation, and manufacturing often have represented efforts by a state to capture a larger share of the market pie. The court has given relatively little weight to such efforts and more to promoting interstate transactions to make the market pie grow. But where environmental and resource controls are at issue, something different is at stake.

Environmental degradation represents a conspicuous form of market failure,[25] a paradigm of problems that cannot be solved and may be only aggravated by increased freedom of trade. To be sure, other forms of regulation and even taxation likewise may be justified on a market-failure rationale. But environmental degradation is widely viewed today as an especially telling instance of market failure, whereas many other forms of regulation have become discredited as instruments of parochial private interests.[26]

An additional and more powerful distinction supports environmental and resource measures: they foster nonmarket values in the natural environment and in associated community cultures. Variety in physical environments and the experiences associated with them, in the patterns and extent of industrial development, and in associated life-styles has been an important part of the geographic and cultural diversity that is a special feature of the United States.[27] Allowing states and localities substantial freedom to limit the development of land and other natural resources in the face of homogenizing development pressures often is calculated to preserve that diversity, and with it a sense of community uniqueness and self-determination. The courts justifiably have been reluctant to treat environmental and land use controls as controls on retail commerce, and thus reduce questions of pristine environments or the maintenance of cultural autonomy to the dollars-and-cents calculus of a national economic marketplace.[28]

Even if there is a special case for local autonomy with respect to land use and other environmental controls, what about the Montana tax case? Is this not simply an effort by a state to capture more of the market pie—an effort that should be judged by traditional standards? While this argument certainly has force, it is nonetheless difficult to distinguish tax measures from regulatory measures to protect environmental and natural resources. Taxes can be used to promote environmental objectives by levying a charge on activities that degrade the environment, and often are preferred by economists to command and control regulation.[29] Ideally, such a tax should be proportional to the amount of degradation caused, but there are many practical difficulties in closely tailoring a charge to the varied effects attributable to, for example, coal mining in different locations and conditions. A flat tax on coal mining is a crude but arguably acceptable substitute. Moreover, it is significant that resources such as coal are nonrenewable and that their exploitation can generate a cycle of boom and bust. Taxing coal exploitation to steady the development process and fund provisions of social infrastructure and alternative long-run employment opportunities serves important community values not fully reflected in the market. As Kneese points out in chapter 4, the Montana tax indeed involved such purposes, accomplished in part through creation of a trust fund.[30]

Congressional Powers

The Supreme Court's refusal to apply undue-burden analysis to resource controversies does not leave a legal void. Congress can deal with interstate natural resource controversies through its powerful battery of legislative powers.

Commerce Power

As an integrated national economy has developed, the courts have upheld an ever broader exercise by Congress of the commerce power, to the point where it now has essentially unlimited power to tax or regulate the development or use of natural resources by private firms, even though their activities occur wholly within one state. For example, in 1981 the Supreme Court upheld congressional authority to require strip mine reclamation in Virginia, even for coal mined and consumed entirely within the state.[31]

By virtue of the Supremacy Clause, Congress' commerce power also has a negative aspect. Congress has essentially unfettered authority to preempt all state regulation of commerce and natural resource development and probably also unlimited authority to preempt state taxation as well. Congress can exercise this preemptive authority to prohibit state measures that differ from federal measures, or it may choose simply to preempt state measures without introducing federal controls, leaving commerce and natural resources free from any regulation or taxation.

Finally, Congress has authority to modify the decisional law developed by federal courts under the Commerce Clause, including the authority to validate state measures that the courts have struck down. And the Commerce Clause also gives Congress effectively unlimited power over the use and apportionment of rivers, lakes, and streams.

Other Powers

Independent of the commerce power, Congress enjoys constitutionally broad authority to manage the vast and resource-rich federal lands—nearly one-third of the nation's total—and to preempt state laws affecting their development. Since the Constitution also gives Congress authority to levy taxes and to spend, it can tax mineral development or the use of common property resources such as air and water, and can use the spending power to help solve pollution and waste disposal problems, to subsidize resource-poor states, or to compensate resource-rich states in return for their acquiescence in federal limitations on their ability to prevent or profit from development.

In recent decades, Congress increasingly has exercised these powers to deal with natural resource development.[32] It has done so by delegating broad responsibility to federal administrative agencies, such as the Departments of Interior and Energy and the Environmental Protection Agency, to regulate particular resources through pollution controls, leasing of federal energy resources, natural gas price regulation, and so on. These broad delegations raise two basic types of legal questions in the context of interstate resource controversies.

First, have the responsible federal administrators properly interpreted and implemented the statutes? The choices presented often involve competing state and regional interests. May the Interior Department lease oil tracts on the Georges Bank off Cape Cod despite environmental risks? May the EPA restrict oil shale development in northwestern Colorado through stringent air pollution control regulations? Litigation challenging federal agency decisions on such controversies has become a battleground for federalism issues.[33]

The second major type of legal problem presented by vague or general statutes is whether such congressional directives and the regulations issued under them preempt state regulation or taxation aimed at the same activity. Does the Atomic Energy Act preempt California's ban on construction of nuclear power plants unless and until nuclear waste disposal problems are solved to California's satisfaction? Do the royalty provisions of the Federal Mineral Leasing Act preclude Montana from imposing a severance tax on the development of federal coal?

In a few instances, Congress explicitly has provided that states may impose measures that are more stringent than those required by federal law. Provisions that explicitly preempt state measures are rare—a reflection of the political ability of the states, through the Congress, to defend their turf. For example, proposals to impose specific limits on the power of states to tax mineral resource development have failed of passage because of opposition in the Senate from energy-rich states.[34] When President Carter's proposed Energy Mobilization Board, which would have had authority to override state procedural rules to expedite development of energy facilities, was blocked in Congress, concern for state autonomy was an important contributor to the result.[35]

Most often, the relevant statute is silent or unclear on the question of preemption, leaving the courts the unenviable responsibility to determine the respective limits of state and federal authority in construing the statute. The results are checkered. For example, courts have held that Washington State's effort to ban jumbo tankers in Puget Sound is preempted by federal law,[36] and that an Interior Department decision to develop federal lands for a given purpose overrides a contrary local zoning regulation.[37] But the dominant, if erratic, tendency of the decisions is against preemption of state law when the federal statute is silent or unclear. For example, in the Montana severance tax case the Supreme Court held that the royalty provisions in the Mineral Leasing Act, which provide for a partial return of federal royalties to the state where the mineral is located, did not preclude Montana's imposition of severance taxes on the same mineral.[38] A federal water project in California has been held subject to a California regulation of water use.[39] And California laws prohibiting further construction of nuclear plants until waste disposal problems have been resolved to the state's satisfaction have been held not preempted by the Atomic Energy Act.[40]

This trend in favor of state autonomy and against federal preemption should be applauded because it helps preserve nonmarket values in local autonomy and environmental diversity. Congress retains ample constitutional authority to override state law to promote energy development or serve other national objectives, but it must do so through explicit legislation that assures political accountability for the decision. Where Congress is silent or fails to reach explicit agreement, the general presumption should favor state autonomy.

Transboundary Nonmarket Impacts

To this point we have focused on state controls or taxes on natural resource development that cause market impacts in other states. Let us turn to the problems presented by nonmarket impacts, the most obvious examples of which are interstate air and water pollution and the appropriation of interstate waters. These resource conflicts have been addressed through federal court jurisdiction to adjudicate controversies to which states are parties, and, in the course of case-by-case decision, a federal common law of interstate conflicts has developed.[41]

Illinois v. Milwaukee

The dispute between Illinois and Wisconsin over the inadequacy of Milwaukee's treatment of sewage discharges into Lake Michigan exemplifies the legal problems raised by interstate spillovers. Illinois invoked the original jurisdiction of the Supreme Court, which held in 1972 that the federal courts could fashion a common law of interstate pollution to decide such controversies.[42] It sent the case back to the lower federal courts for decision in the first instance.

Should Milwaukee be required to spend hundreds of millions of dollars to prevent sewer overflows and treat its sewage to a greater degree? How serious are the impacts of its discharges on the health of swimmers on Chicago beaches? The Supreme Court left these questions to the lower federal courts, which concluded that substantial additional controls were necessary.

The case reached the Supreme Court again in the fourth case involving interstate resource conflicts decided by the Justices during the Court's 1980 term.[43] This time the Court held that the entire controversy fell under the 1972 Federal Water Pollution Control Act, which preempted federal judge-made law of interstate pollution. Hence, Illinois must seek its remedy, if any, from the federal EPA and not by direct litigation in the federal courts.

I find the decision unsatisfactory. It relies upon the system of regulation introduced by Congress in 1972 and administered by the EPA, a system that does not really meet the concerns raised by Illinois in the litigation. The 1972 Act essentially aims at ensuring that all municipalities adopt a minimum, nationally uniform level of pollution control.[44] But Illinois' complaint was that this minimum level did not ensure adequate water quality in the particular situation presented in Lake Michigan. Also, the EPA, like other federal agencies, is reluctant to take on heated controversies between states.

This case typifies the problems of relying on Congress and federal administrators, who have strong incentives to adopt uniform measures that do not come to grips with such special local or regional problems as acid rain or ozone transport. Congress operates under norms of reciprocity that make adoption of nonuniform measures difficult, and representatives are reluctant to delegate broad discretion to administrators to impose nonuniform measures that would provide economic advantage to certain states or regions. Administrators favor uniformity in order to reduce decision-making costs and political controversy.

Unwarranted Deference

In its second *Illinois* v. *Milwaukee* opinion, the Court emphasized the limitations of judges and the adversary process of proof in dealing with complex engineering and scientific issues. It also stressed the lack of any clear benchmarks for the value choices that must be made in deciding how much the taxpayers of Milwaukee (and the federal government) must spend in order to reduce certain hazards in waters adjacent to Illinois. As we have seen, courts do have limited competence to deal with issues like acid rain, but unless they take on interstate spillover problems, inertia or political clout may prevent Congress from filling the gap.

For example, the Clean Air Act must be amended to address specifically the problem of acid rain—preferably, in my opinion, through a system of market-based incentives that would stimulate cost-minimizing reductions of sulfur emissions over a broad area. But the political muscle of the midwestern industries and states apparently responsible for much acid rain may be sufficient to block innovative legislation. Moreover, unlike the usual situation of natural resource regulation or taxation, this is not a case where nonmarket values are best promoted by judicial restraint. Freedom to pollute another state's air not only generates economically wasteful externalities, but also destroys that state's ability to pursue nonmarket values in the management of its own resources. Accordingly, while I welcome the Court's deference to state natural resource taxation and regulation under the Commerce Clause, I conclude that its retreat from deciding interstate spillover controversies is unwarranted.

Nonmarket interstate impacts other than pollution spillovers present serious institutional problems. Two are especially worrisome: the preservation of exceptional scenic resources and the disposal of toxic wastes.

Scenic Values

One set of problems stems from the national interest in preserving scenic areas of exceptional beauty for the benefit of all citizens, including future generations. If states are left free to make natural resource decisions, they may be led by economic forces to destroy these scenic assets, depriving citizens of other states of access to them. Strong market forces operate on states to assure that weight is given to national interests in energy development, but market incentives—principally, the economic interest in tourism—to preserve high-quality environments are too weak to assure that long-run national interests in preservation are served adequately. Utah's efforts to promote a massive strip-mined coal project within plain view of Bryce Canyon National Park illustrates the depth of the problem.

Toxic Waste Disposal

A second set of problems is posed by the need to find acceptable disposal sites for toxic and radioactive wastes. If states with the most suitable sites refuse to allow disposal within their borders, citizens in other states may be exposed to hazards resulting from unsuitable or illegal disposal efforts.

The combination of state autonomy and market forces does not deal adequately with such problems. Congressional regulation also is ill-suited because these problems call for nonuniform, nonreciprocal outcomes: some states must forgo economic development of pristine areas or accept hazardous wastes for the benefit of other states. Congress has great difficulty in mandating such outcomes, as the history of radioactive waste disposal illustrates.[45] Indeed, as Kneese points out in the previous chapter, disposal is by no means a problem-free process even when the state in principle agrees to it.

The federal courts likewise are ill-suited to deal with such problems. In deciding interstate pollution controversies, they can draw on principles of nuisance and tort developed over centuries. But there is no precedent, no experience, no principled basis on which courts could require one state, at the behest of other states, to forgo development of a scenic resource or accept hazardous wastes for disposal.[46]

New Institutions Needed

All of this suggests the need for novel institutions to deal with this class of problems. Let me note some possible candidates.

Legislation is a form of bargaining and Congress is in a position to provide for what economists call side payments through the exercise of its taxing and spending powers. In the past, western states have received heavy federal subsidies for water and other developments. These subsidies may be understood as an implicit side payment for federal government control of many of the resources within their borders through ownership of the public lands. The trick today is to find an environmentally more benign form of side payment as a quid pro quo for forgoing development of scenic areas or accepting hazardous wastes. What about, for example, a federally funded trust fund, analogous to the Montana coal tax trust fund, to support development of environmentally benign industry and agriculture?[47]

Another approach is the development of new institutions to select locations that should be called upon to bear burdens in the national interest. New mechanisms for joint federal and state decision making have been explored in the context of nuclear waste disposal. Examples include a site selection "jury" that would include representatives of affected states,[48] and a structured process of consultation and concurrence involving state representatives, federal agencies, Congress, and the president in a prescribed sequence.[49] A different approach was authorized by Congress for the Low-Level Radioactive Waste Policy Act of 1980,[50] which establishes a baseline "policy" that each state shall dispose of low-level wastes generated within its borders and then authorizes and provides federal planning support for regional disposal schemes through interstate compacts. These innovations deserve wider attention and application.

Dialectical Federalism

Higher energy prices, environmental concerns, pressures to develop the West, acid rain, and hazardous wastes are not going to go away. In addressing such problems, the dialectic of federalism must address not only the respective claims of centralization and decentralization, but also the need to strike a balance between market and nonmarket values.

Nonmarket values have become more precious because of the whole range of forces discussed throughout this book. It is hardly surprising that the judicial techniques developed to maintain an open-market economy cannot be carried over to environmental and natural resource controversies where, to a considerable extent, the market has been and must be rejected as an appropriate basis for resource allocation.

In some areas, these considerations counsel judicial retreat. The courts, I have argued, should not, in the absence of discrimination, invalidate state regulation or taxation of natural resource development as an unconstitutional burden on interstate commerce. They also should decline to hold that such measures are preempted by federal law unless Congress expressly so provides. But in other contexts, such as interstate pollution, I have argued that courts should take the lead in confronting problems that cannot simply be left to the states or Congress. In still other areas, including preservation of scenic resources and hazardous waste disposal, new institutional approaches seem needed.

The dialectic of federalism is not fixed. Our federal system, like the law itself, presents a paradox: it must be continuously transformed in order to endure.

Notes

1. This view of trade relations under the Articles of Confederation is recounted in G. Reynolds, *The Distribution of Power to Regulate Interstate Carriers Between the Nations and the States* (New York, Columbia University Press, 1928); and in C. Nettels, *The Emergence of a National Economy 1775–1815* (New York, Holt, Rinehart and Winston, 1962) pp. 69–75 and 90–92. The traditional view has recently been subject to strong criticism. See E. Kitch, "Regulation and the American Common Market," in D. Tarlock, ed., *Regulation, Federalism, and Interstate Commerce* (Cambridge, Mass., Oelgeschlager, Gunn & Hain, 1981), and the sources there discussed. The criticism is that the limited amount of interstate trade during the Confederation was attributable to the underdeveloped state of the economy, and that there is no substantial evidence that state taxes and regulations posed a serious obstacle to such trade. Just as the traditional view exalts national regulatory power, so the criticism reflects suspicion of central governmental power or a belief in the benign power of market forces.

2. See note 1; and F. Ribble, *State and National Power over Commerce* (New York, Columbia University Press, 1937) pp. 3–4; *H. P. Hood & Sons v. DuMond*, 336 U.S. 525, (1949) p. 533 and sources there cited; *Hughes v. Oklahoma*, 441 U.S. 322, (1979) pp. 325–326. See also *American Can Co. v. Oregon Liquor Control Commission*, 517 P., 2d 691, 696 Ore. App. (1973), *review denied, id.* at 691 (Ore. 1974).

3. Alexander Hamilton, *The Federalist* no. 22. Article I also provides that "(No) State shall, without the consent of Congress, lay any Imposts or Duties on Imports or Exports, except what may be absolutely necessary for executing its inspection laws."

4. L. Farrand, *The Records of the Federal Convention* (New Haven, Conn., Yale University Press, 1937) p. 515 (July 2), see also the statement of Governor Randolph, 26 (May 17).

5. *The Federalist* no. 80.

6. See generally, F. Zimmerman and M. Wendell, *The Law and Use of Interstate Compacts* (Lexington, Ky., Council of State Governments, 1976).

7. See, for example, *Toomer v. Witsell*, 334 U.S. 385 (1948); *Hincklin v. Orbech*, 437 U.S. 518 (1978) on hiring preference for state's citizens in exploitation of state's resources. However, differential fish and game license fees for residents and nonresidents have been sustained where justified by residents' tax contributions. See *Baldwin v. Montana Fish & Wildlife Commission*, 436 U.S. 371 (1978).

8. States, not regions, are the entities recognized by the law. It is the laws of states and their political subdivisions which are subject to legal challenge under the Commerce and Privileges and Immunities clauses. States and their political subdivisions are the parties to invoke the federal courts' jurisdiction to resolve interstate disputes. States are the parties to interstate compacts. Regions as such are without legal standing.

9. See generally, Ernest J. Brown, "Justice Frankfurter—The Open Economy," *Yale Law Journal* 67 (1957) p. 219.

10. See generally, L. Tribe, *American Constitutional Law* (Mineola, N.Y., Foundation Press, 1978) pp. 340-368.

11. *H. P. Hood and Sons v. DuMond*, 336 U.S. 525 (1949). Should we accept this self-congratulatory conclusion? If one believes that the free movement of capital and labor operates powerfully to undermine state trade barriers and maintain an open market, then

the contributions of the judges may be comparatively minor. See Kitch, "Regulation." The lack in the reported cases of egregious state efforts to balkanize the economy may help support the economic thesis, but it may also reflect the deterrent effect of judicial precedent on state legislation.

12. There were, however, a number of earlier decisions, most of them involving efforts by a state to reserve natural resources such as natural gas or game for consumption by its own citizens. See, for example, *West* v. *Kansas Natural Gas Co.*, 221 U.S. 229 (1911), concerning natural gas; *Geer* v. *Connecticut*, 161 U.S. 519 (1896), concerning game.

13. 101 S.Ct. 3075 (1981). See also *New England Power Co.* v. *New Hampshire*, 102 S.Ct. 1096 (1982), invalidating New Hampshire's efforts to reserve for its citizens all of the economic benefits accruing from generation of hydroelectric power within the state.

14. It also should be noted that the gas was taken from Outer Continental Shelf lands and was passing through Louisiana en route to the ultimate consumers. Louisiana thus was exploiting its strategic location athwart the flow of commerce in a manner like that attributed to New York and other port states under the Articles of Confederation.

15. See *Pennsylvania* v. *West Virginia*, 262 U.S. 553 (1923), concerning natural gas; *Hughes* v. *Oklahoma*, 441 U.S. 322 (1979), concerning game; *City of Altus* v. *Carr*, 385 U.S. 35 (1966) *aff'd per curiam* 255 F. Supp. 828 (W.D. Tex. 1966), concerning groundwater.

16. *City of Philadelphia* v. *New Jersey*, 437 U.S. 617 (1978).

17. See, for example, *Dean Milk Co.* v. *City of Madison*, 340 U.S. 349 (1951); *Southern Pacific Co.* v. *Arizona*, 325 U.S. 761 (1945).

18. 101 S. Ct. 2946 (1981).

19. Compare *Exxon Corp.* v. *Wisconsin Department of Revenue*, 100 S. Ct. 2109 (1980), sustaining a Wisconsin tax apportionment formula that includes a share of Exxon's profits from crude oil extraction in other states.

20. 101 S. Ct. 715 (1981)

21. See, for example, *Reserve Mining Co.* v. *United States*, 498 F. 2d. 1073 (8th Cir. 1974).

22. See Charles E. McClure, "Tax Exporting and the Commerce Clause; Reflections on *Commonwealth Edison*," Paper presented at Lincoln Land Institute Conference on Fiscal Federalism and the Taxation of Natural Resources, Cambridge, Massachusetts, 1981.

23. See, for example, *Roe* v. *Wade*, 410 U.S. 113 (1973).

24. For example, Montana and Wyoming alone contain 68 percent of the nation's low-sulfur coal reserves. *Commonwealth Edison Co.* v. *Montana*, 101 S. Ct. 2946, 2965 n.l. (Justice Blackmun dissenting) (1981).

25. See generally, Richard B. Stewart and James E. Krier, *Environmental Law and Policy* (2 ed., Indianapolis, Ind., Bobbs-Merrill, 1978) chapter 4.

26. Three to four decades ago, the problem of excess capacity was viewed as perhaps the most threatening form of market failure, a perception undoubtedly influential in persuading courts to uphold state price-fixing and market allocation systems against Commerce Clause attack without inquiry whether the local benefits outweighed the burdens imposed upon out-of-state consumers. See, for example, *Milk Control Bd.* v. *Eisenberg Farm Prods.*, 306 U.S. 346 (1939), concerning milk price controls; *Cities Serv. Co.* v. *Peerless Oil & Gas Co.*, 340 U.S. 179 (1950), concerning natural gas price controls. In recent years, however, the "cut-throat competition" rationale for government intervention has lost much of its persuasiveness. See Stephen G. Breyer, "Analyzing Regulatory Failure: Mismatches, Less Restrictive Alternatives, and Reform," *Harvard Law Review* vol. 92 (1979) pp. 547, 556-557, 587-590. In *Federal Power Comm'n* v. *Corporation Comm'n*,

362 F. supp. 522 (W.D. Okla. 1973), *aff'd.* 415 U.S. 961 (1974), the court invalidated, on alternate Commerce Clause and preemption grounds, a natural gas price-fixing scheme similar to the one sustained in *Peerless*. Courts accordingly appear more willing to uphold without scrutiny into benefits and burdens those state interventions that are directed at forms of market failure contemporaneously viewed as compelling.

27. See Richard B. Stewart, "The Development of Administrative and Quasi-Constitutional Law in Judicial Review of Environmental Decisionmaking: Lessons from the Clean Air Act, *Iowa Law Review* 62 (1977) p. 714. Compare with J. Sax, *Mountains Without Handrails* (Ann Arbor, University of Michigan Press, 1980), which justifies maintenance of pristine environments in order to develop noncommercial *individual* sensibilities.

28. The conclusion suggested by the Court's decisions is that so long as a state relies on market ordering as the basic form of economic organization, it must be prepared to provide substantial justification for any restrictions upon the free flow of resources and commodities throughout the nation. But if it decides to withhold resources (including energy minerals or air) from commercial exploitation altogether in order to pursue nonmarket values, only minimal justification is required.

29. See Frederick R. Anderson, Allen V. Kneese, Philip D. Reed, Serge Taylor, and Russell B. Stevenson, *Environmental Improvement Through Economic Incentives* (Baltimore, Md., Johns Hopkins University Press for Resources for the Future, 1978); Allen V. Kneese and Charles L. Schultze, *Pollution, Prices, and Public Policy* (Washington, D.C., The Brookings Institution, 1975). For discussion of some of the difficulties in setting a severance tax equal to the social costs imposed by extraction of energy resources, see Note, "An Outline for Development of Cost-Based State Severance Taxes," *Natural Resources Journal* vol. 20 (1980) p. 913.

30. Under the Montana Constitution, at least 50 percent of the severance tax revenues must be paid into a permanent trust fund, the principal of which may be appropriated only by vote of three-fourths of each house of the state legislature.

The Province of Alberta has a multibillion-dollar trust fund founded on oil and gas revenues. For discussion of some of the problems in implementing the trust fund concept, see "The Alberta Heritage Savings Trust Fund: An Overview of the Issues," *Canadian Public Policy/Analyse de Politiques* (suppl. issue, 1980) p. 6.

31. *Hodel* v. *Virginia Surface Mining & Reclamation Association,* 101 S. Ct. 2352 (1981). *Hodel* makes clear that *National League of Cities* v. *Usery,* 426 U.S. 833 (1976), which invalidated—as violative of the Tenth Amendment and principles of federalism—the application of federal minimum wage requirements to state employees, does not limit federal regulation of private activity even though it supersedes or preempts state regulatory measures.

32. The relation between federal court decisions invalidating state measures under the Commerce Clause and the emergence of federal regulation has recently attracted scholarly attention. It has been suggested that federal regulation emerges because federal Commerce Clause decisions frustrate state responses to regulatory demands, and that this is often undesirable because regulation is often economically inefficient and that, further, state regulation is less effective than federal because of the mobility of labor and capital across state boundaries. See E. Kitch, "Regulation;" T. Daintith and S. Williams, "Energy-related Natural Resources: An 'Acute Problem' of Integration," paper presented at Conference on European Legal Integration in Light of the American Federal Experience, Florence, Italy, 1981. This thesis finds no support in the field examined here. Federal regulation has arisen despite the fact that state regulation generally has not been invalidated by the federal courts. In those areas where state measures have been struck down (as in the case of bans on game, natural gas, and water export), equivalent federal regulation has not been forthcoming. The development of federal price controls on natural

gas represents a potential exception to this conclusion. See Daintith and Williams, pp. 86–102, although the principal impetus for federal regulation in that context would have been the inability of energy-consuming states to impose minimum price controls.

The pattern with respect to environmental controls is more consistent with the thesis that even though state environmental regulations may be upheld by federal courts, states that desire high environmental quality will be reluctant to adopt strong environmental regulations because the natural market system makes industry in such states vulnerable to input competition from firms in states with lax environmental controls. States desiring stronger environmental controls therefore seek imposition by the federal government of stringent, uniform controls on all states. See T. Heller, "The Economic Impact of Trans-nationalism/Federalism: The Mutual Impact of Legal and Economic Integration," Paper presented at Conference on European Legal Integration in Light of the American Federal Experience, Florence, Italy, 1981.

33. See generally, Stewart and Krier, *Environmental Law,* chap. 5 and 7.

34. *Business Week,* February 16, 1981, p. 26.

35. See "The Energy Mobilization Board," in "Developments: Energy Law and the Environment," *Ecology Law Quarterly* vol. 8 (1980) pp. 725 and 727.

36. *Ray* v. *Atlantic Richfield Co.,* 435 U.S. 151 (1978).

37. *Ventura County* v. *Gulf Oil Corp.,* 601 F. 2d 1080 (9th Cir. 1979).

38. See 101 S. Ct. at 2961–64.

39. *California* v. *United States,* 438 U.S. 645 (1978).

40. *Pacific Legal Foundation* v. *State Energy Resources Commission,* 16 ERC 1513 (9th Cir. 1981).

41. Most interstate conflicts have been reviewed by the Supreme Court, exercising its original jurisdiction to resolve controversies between states. In addition, the Supreme Court has held that the lower courts have authority to apply the federal common law of interstate conflicts under their federal question jurisdiction. Finally, the Supreme Court has ruled that Congress has implicit constitutional authority to enact statutes to govern the resolution of such disputes, and in so doing, to preempt the judge-made common law of interstate disputes. See P. Bator, P. Mishkin, D. Shapiro, and H. Wechsler, *Hart and Wechsler's The Federal Courts and the Federal System* (2 ed., Mineola, N.Y., The Foundation Press, 1973) pp. 264–267.

42. *Illinois* v. *Milwaukee,* 406 U.S. 91 (1972)

43. *Milwaukee* v. *Illinois,* 101 S. Ct. 1784 (1981).

44. See Stewart and Krier, *Environmental Law,* pp. 505–507.

45. See R. Smith, "Strategies for Siting Nuclear Waste Repositories," Ph.D. Thesis, Harvard University, 1981.

46. But see *Sierra Club* v. *Ruckelshaus,* 344 F. Supp. 253 (D.D.C.) *aff'd per curiam,* 4ERC 1205 (D.C.Cu.); *aff'd* by an equally divided Court, 412 U.S. 541 (1973) interpreting the Clean Air Act to include a principle of nondegradation prohibiting states with pristine environments from substantially degrading air quality. The justifications for the decision are examined in Stewart, "The Development of Administrative and Quasi-Constitutional Law."

47. Already the federal government returns at least half of its royalties from the leasing of public lands to the states in which the leased lands are located. Mineral Lands Leasing Act, 30 U.S.C. 191 (1976)

48. See K. Lee, "A Federalist Strategy for Nuclear Waste Management," *Science* vol. 208 (1980) p. 679.

49. See the Interagency Review Group on Nuclear Waste Management, *Report to the President,* TID-29442 (1979); S. 742, 98th Cong. (1979).

50. 94 Stat. 3347, 42 U.S.C. 2021b.

chapter six

Externality, Conflict, and Decision

Clifford S. Russell

In describing a number of regional conflicts over resources or the environment, the first four chapters allow the inference that our collective decision-making and enforcing institutions do not always deal very successfully with such conflicts.[1] Indeed, in some cases the institutions may create or be the problem. These conclusions are reinforced by Stewart's examination of those institutions in the previous chapter. His suggestion that their reappraisal is in order in light of current and inevitable future conflicts seems to me most sensible. In this chapter I suggest a few directions that a reappraisal might explore. I also believe, however, that we should first try to be clearer about the nature of the conflicts we observe and about whether collective decisions and actions are necessary, or even desirable, as part of "solutions" to those conflicts.

Resource and environmental conflicts might be categorized in any number of ways—for example, by the resource commodity or environmental medium involved, the forum(s) in which the issue is being fought, the number of parties involved, or the homogeneity of the regional interests at stake. I propose to adopt and extend a categorization used implicitly or explicitly elsewhere in this volume. It is based on the notion of *externality*, a jargon word of economics that was introduced by Kneese in chapter 4. Inasmuch as what follows leans rather heavily on this concept, however, I ask the reader's indulgence if I once again set forth some basic definitions.

Three Kinds of Externality

The term *externality* applies generally to situations in which firm (or individual) A creates through its activities a cost or a benefit for firm (or individual) B but does not take this cost or benefit into account in making its decisions about its own production or consumption. Two sorts of externalities and thus, by implication, two sources of conflict, usually are distinguished.[2] *Pecuniary externalities* involve market interactions, as when the advent of a competing source of supply drives down the price an existing firm can charge for its product. Of course, such effects are the stuff of economic growth and change. (Thus it is that economists often prefix "mere" to pecuniary.) *Real externalities* involve direct interactions, through competition for a common property resource such as an oil field, for example, or through upstream water pollution and downstream water supply withdrawals.

To these two sources of conflict I propose to add a third, which I call *political externalities*. I apply this term both to situations in which the design (constitution) of our political institutions creates conflicts by excluding from collective decisions the voices of legitimately interested parties, and to situations in which the decisions or actions themselves prevent the resolution of conflicts arising from another type of externality. In a case offered by Stewart, for example, a political externality would arise if a state decided to develop a resource and in the process to scar a wilderness or scenic area valued by residents of other states. The design of jurisdictions and decision processes based on residence means that the resulting conflict is not just between groups of individuals, but also between excluded groups and a state or states. A slightly different form of political externality arises when political acts place barriers in the way of bargaining and compensation that might have allowed resolution of actual or potential conflicts, as when a state closes its radioactive waste disposal sites rather than bargain over terms on which it will accept waste from other states.

By way of further clarification, consider what types of externality potentially are involved in extreme state decisions about environmental quality or resource use. (The possibility of extreme decisions often is cited as a reason for uniform national laws. Existing laws strictly limit the scope for such contrasting policies, but the examples still are valuable, if hypothetical.) First consider a decision by a state to opt for very low environmental quality and, one assumes, high employment and money incomes. Assuming the state to be the decision unit, what types of externalities, and what sources of conflict are involved?

- A (negative) pecuniary externality is created because the state will lower the costs of polluting firms operating within its borders. This will raise their profits relative to firms operating elsewhere and will in the longer run encourage firms to migrate to it.
- A new or increased (and negative) real externality will exist if the increase in pollution spills over into other states.
- A (negative) political externality is created if residents of other states directly value the environmental quality within the deciding state.

The opposite extreme decision—to opt for very high environmental quality—creates the opposite signed externalities. In the next several pages I will discuss these externalities and attached conflicts as collective decision problems—whether they are such problems and, if so, what has been tried in dealing with them. I conclude with a few suggestions for different approaches.

First, however, let me dispose of the idea that there is something intrinsically wrong with a system that allows externality-creating decisions to be made. There is no perfect system of geographic jurisdictional lines; that is, no system exists that prevents all negative externalities while giving to well-defined local majorities the right to have their preferences honored.[3] A unitary or completely centralized and uniform system eliminates local choices in the interests of eliminating externalities. A system of complete "states' rights" emphasizes local choice while risking externalities and conflict.

Given that any real system has to balance these competing ends, what institutions are—or, in theory, should be—available for deciding matters of conflict?

Pecuniary Externalities

We should be wary of assuming that a collective decision problem is involved at all in cases of pecuniary externality. As noted, these external effects are the signals that drive the continuous adjustment process that is a market economy. They most often are thought of as transmitting changes in tastes, technology, or resource availability, but a state government's decision to change its policy on resource exploitation or on environmental quality certainly can be ranked with these other items as an "exogenous shock" to the system. To the extent that we try to stop a signal by stopping a pecuniary externality we block adjustments to changes in reality.

In fact, adjustments to pecuniary externalities in the U.S. economy are made by *mobile* firms and individuals. While a few caveats are set out below, the general proposition is that pecuniary externalities take care of themselves as these firms and individuals shift locations and types of activities in response to changing wages, prices, and profit potential. When the ability of economic agents to move about and change industries, production processes, and so forth, is seen to be inextricably combined with the movement of political actors (voters), the range of possible adjustments to state decisions imposing pecuniary externalities appears formidable. Thus, individuals can choose the balance of environmental quality and money income they want from among those "on offer" by the several states.

But this is not the only point: when a state changes the balance it offers, it invites shifts in population and economic activity that both take advantage of the new opportunity and tend to reduce the differences, at least in money income, between that state and the others. For example, if a policy of maintaining low environmental quality really does raise wages for workers and profits for the firms of state A, the following reactions can be expected.

- Some out-of-state firms will move in, bidding up the price of labor, land, and perhaps other inputs and thus eating into differential profits.
- Some citizens of other states will move in to pick up higher wages and in the process will put downward pressure on those wage rates.
- Some citizens of state A will emigrate to seek a balance of environmental quality and money incomes more to their liking.

- Some firms located in state A may move out because the higher pollution levels affect their costs of production or because their labor force is disproportionately (in numbers or power) represented in the emigrants.

In short, pecuniary externalities created by state resource and environmental policies impose costs internally as well as externally. And the gains they apparently create can neither be confined to the state's citizens at the time of the policy change nor, indeed, guaranteed in the longer run in the face of individual adjustments.

How About Severance Taxes?

Similar reasoning should carry us beyond the notion that a western state's severance tax on energy resources somehow is a momentous public problem. How can this be? What about the residents of, say, Massachusetts, who have to pay higher electricity rates because of Montana's coal tax?

If, as suggested strongly in earlier chapters, the tax represents a capture of rents accruing to high-quality and low-cost deposits (relative to the marginal suppliers of coal), the existence of the tax actually means nothing to the price. Montana coal would cost the same if the state tax went to zero (or, more realistically, to the level of the lowest state severance tax). Only the recipients of the rent would be different.

Also, no one is forced to live in Massachusetts or any part of the Northeast for that matter. But many of us who have done so consider that the cost, in terms of cold winters and high energy prices, is balanced by cooler summers, wonderful scenery, and other amenities both physical and cultural. Those who disagree can and do move to Montana or New Mexico or Florida.[4]

Moreover, the citizens of Massachusetts can and do collectively capture a portion of the rents generated by *their* unique, immobile resources—the beaches of Cape Cod, the forests of the Berkshires, and so forth. Montanans who want to enjoy these resources pay for the privilege, not only to private owners, innkeepers, and service stations, but to the state at large through sales, lodging, and entertainment taxes.

Finally, coal production is immobile only in the short or intermediate run. If, in fact, a state's taxes reduce the rents accruing to owners to unacceptably low levels, exploration, development, and mining activities will shift elsewhere. Only if *all* the out-of-state coal deposits already have been discovered is exploration irrelevant. And even if that were true, the balancing of total costs—including price, transportation, and cost of use in power plants—still would assure significant potential competition for western coal.

Dealing With Objections

Many of the caveats promised above already will have occurred to the reader as objections to this sanguine view of a flexible and changing economy. Consider only four.

Most important, this is a long-run view and ignores the painful disruptions of the short run. To combine two aphorisms: the short run always is with us, and in the long run we all are dead. What good, then, is a long-run view? The point is that we should apply our collective ingenuity to ameliorating the short-run problems and smoothing the path of adjustment, rather than struggling to stop or forbid the changes themselves. The version of this problem discussed here probably is much less important than the version posed as technology changes, entire industries die and new ones are born. But the Luddite response is no less inappropriate.

A second caveat or objection—and a good one—is that I have ignored the possibility of state monopoly or strong oligopoly position. A state that has a monopoly position in a resource indeed should not be allowed to exploit it without limit. But as a practical matter this is very seldom, if ever, the case. It certainly is not the case for Montana coal.[5] (It might be the case that there are only a very few states with naturally occurring very deep harbors, but even here, substitutes such as dredged channels and offshore "ports" are available at finite cost.) We should try to avoid seeing a monopolist behind every price increase.

Third, states may create barriers to entry by firms or individuals and thus complicate and brake the adjustment process. It is true, for example, that Alaska's government passed a law tying a citizen's share in the state's oil revenue to length of state residence.[6] Oregon and Washington seem to have at least semiofficial policies of discouraging in-migration by those who would share in the high environmental quality of the Pacific Northwest. As an economist, I am not equipped to say

whether serious efforts to interfere with migration of people and businesses ever can be constitutional, but it seems unlikely. Finally, consider
three more specific objections arising from concerns about equity.

- Poor people cannot afford to move, and thus policies of the sort I
  blithely have accepted will lead to a widening of regional income
  differentials and, at the extreme, to a Northeast entirely populated
  by welfare families. This argument simply is not valid, however
  much it may appeal to our egalitarian instincts. Many of the existing
  welfare families in the Northeast moved from the South and Puerto
  Rico in response to income signals. In fact, it may be easier for
  people without home ownership worries to move.

- New England, say, offers a unique life-style and people should not
  be forced (or even expected) to leave it for mere money income.
  But no one is forced to do anything, and neither should the nation
  at large be forced to subsidize a style of life in the face of funda-
  mental changes that make it more expensive to maintain.

- What about interest rates and housing prices? Briefly, it would be
  remarkable if the current situation, with real short-term interest
  rates of around 9 or 10 percent, lasted very long. Again, it seems
  short-sighted to make policy to accommodate a particular aberra-
  tion.

Real Externalities

The adjective "real" certainly hints that one cannot dismiss this source
of conflict as easily as pecuniary effects. Indeed, it commonly is accepted
that real externalities (nearly always) are proper matters for collective
decision and action.[7] The usual situation assumed in economics involves
private "emitters" of the externality and other private "receptors," all
operating within a single political jurisdiction. But taking the state as
the decision unit, and viewing the situation as one in which one state's
policy creates a real spillover into another state or states, it becomes
even more obvious that decentralized bargaining among (or other actions by) private firms and individuals cannot be counted on to solve
the problem. The underlying conflict may be between individuals in one
state and the government of another state, but the most significant such

items seem to reach the public stage as conflicts between states.

How then does our system attempt to deal with interstate conflicts stemming from real externalities—pollution spillovers, upstream water consumption, or oil field or aquifer management, for example? One possibility is for interstate bargaining to take place, either *ad hoc* or in the context of a continuing forum. The first, as Stewart points out, is a weak reed.[8] States have little to bargain with outside of the logrolling possibilities of multipurpose legislatures. Simple side payments, such as those mentioned by Kneese in the Rhine and Colorado rivers context, seem to be difficult to justify politically, perhaps because they are so easily referred to as "bribes," with all the underhandedness that connotes.

Regional Institutions

It long has been a popular idea among economists and engineers that formalizing and making permanent the bargaining situation, as through a multistate river basin commission, improves the bargaining process.[9] The experience of the Delaware River Basin Commission (DRBC) in deciding on an ambient water quality standard for that river often has been cited as an example of what can be accomplished by regional "problem shed" institutions.[10] Indeed, this form of activity is explicitly encouraged by the federal Clean Water Act (Section 103, "Interstate Cooperation and Uniform Laws").

Without wishing to denigrate the real accomplishments of the DRBC or its descendents, I do wish to suggest skepticism of the general claim. For one thing, problem sheds for other externalities are not so easy to define. This is most obviously true for air pollution, whether local or long distance.[11] And it is true as well for such common property spillover problems as fisheries management.[12]

Regional institutions, at least as the country so far has tried them, also suffer from constitutional infirmities that largely are attributable to the jealous guarding of powers by states and national governments (or state and local governments, if that situation applies).[13] As creatures of treaties between states, regional bodies do not reflect one decision-affecting vote per X-thousand voters, but one vote per state. Clearly, the affected population in each state may be very different and there also will be varying amounts of unaffected territory and associated population across the compacting states.

For the most part, these institutions do not have independent powers to tax and spend, and often seem to lack power to enforce their decisions. For a regional government to have such power would require that—like a state—it be legitimately structured on the lines of equal representation. And state and national power would be by some perceptible amount diminished. But in the absence of such powers, regional bodies will have trouble dealing with situations in which the benefits and costs of plausible solutions are not roughly evenly shared, as models suggest they were on the Delaware estuary *water* quality case.[14] The question of compensation or cost sharing will loom larger when the problem is one of upstream discharge (or water use, as in the Colorado) and downstream damages (or forgone use). Finally, of course, it is mildly appalling to think of creating a special set of regional governments to deal with every real externality problem.

Recourse to the Courts

If bargaining fails, legal action is possible. Thus, New Jersey sued New York City and State in 1929 to prevent construction of water supply reservoirs on the upper Delaware River and its tributaries that were designed to divert 600 million gallons per day (mgd) to New York City and therefore out of the Delaware Basin. The decision in this case allowed New York to proceed but reduced the allowed diversion to 440 mgd and set up a system to protect the flow in the lower river during drought periods.[15] In 1974 Vermont sued New York State and International Paper Company over discharges from the company's plant at Ticonderoga into the narrow upper part of Lake Champlain, the boundary of the two states. Another example of recourse to the courts is *Illinois* v. *Milwaukee*, to which Stewart already has referred.

In Stewart's opinion, the courts increasingly are reluctant to decide the merits of such cases, recognizing their lack of technical expertise (although special masters can be used, as in *Vermont* v. *New York*), as well as their potential political vulnerability. In this context, however, it is interesting that the courts were very reluctant to allow other fruit-growing states to protect themselves, by quarantines and embargoes, from the threat of Mediterranean fruit fly invasion from California during the summer of 1981. Specifically, Florida and Texas quarantine provisions were struck down by federal district courts.[16] Whatever the technical and equitable merits of the decisions, at least decisions were made promptly when promptness was required. The Supreme Court, in contrast, "postponed" consideration of the case, thus by default leaving the threatened states without quarantines.[17]

Recall from chapter 5 that the way out chosen by the Court in *Illinois v. Milwaukee* was to point to the administrative remedies available under the Clean Water Act. Both this law and the Clean Air Act were designed to eliminate significant interstate pollution externalities through technologically specified discharge limitations supplemented by ambient quality standards (but both provide some backup procedures through which the Environmental Protection Agency can adjudicate any remaining interstate squabbles).[18] In fact, of course, long-range air pollution transport problems—acid rain in particular—raise significant interstate issues that are not addressed by the Clean Air Act's emphasis on local air quality. More generally, any system of emission limitations based on a standard technology or on allowable discharges per ton of product or throughput will run into trouble as population rises and production levels increase.

Moreover, the EPA's actions and statements in two interstate air pollution proceedings suggest that the Reagan administration is at least as chary as the courts of stepping into the middle of an interstate conflict. In the agency's first major decision in an interstate air pollution dispute, EPA Administrator Gorsuch proposed to deny that a power plant in Indiana "cause(s) or substantially contribute(s) to a violation of the SO_2 NAAQS [National Ambient Air Quality Standard] in Kentucky. . . ."[19] In the larger case of a petition by New York and Pennsylvania directed against Ohio, procedural requirements introduced by the EPA seem to some observers to make it almost impossible for one or more states to obtain a finding that specific sources are creating an interstate violation.[20]

One cannot help but agree with Stewart that existing options for dealing with interstate conflicts over real externalities, while partly effective in some cases, do not seem very robust. If disputes become technically more complex, potentially more expensive, with no intrinsically equal sharing of costs and benefits, these institutions may prove very frustrating indeed.

Political Externalities

It should not be surprising that mechanisms for dealing with interstate political externalities are more blunt, *ad hoc,* and primitive than those institutions just discussed in the context of real spillovers. This is partly a matter of definition; if good mechanisms existed for bringing all relevant interests into the collective consideration of resource and environmental disputes, there would be no such animal as a political externality.

The nation nevertheless does try to come to grips with political externalities, recognizing that they can be responsible for serious tensions. For example, individuals and firms are allowed to contribute to state political campaigns in states of which they are not citizens or in which they do not operate. But this is a highly imperfect way of gaining a voice. It even may be counterproductive if out-of-state support becomes important enough that some candidates can be branded as carpetbaggers.

Other possibilities exist in the legal and administrative arenas for out-of-state voices to be heard. For example, a national environmental group may claim standing in an intrastate dispute on the basis of having members in the state, however few they may be. It also is possible for outside groups or individuals to find inside allies (local environmental groups, for example) who can be supported with money and expertise. Again, however, local resentment can be generated by such intervention, so that the "right" is certainly, if somewhat vaguely, circumscribed.

When all else fails, or when a number of similar disputes make it seem an efficient and promising tactic, political externalities at the state level often are "solved" by dragging them up to the federal level by suitable publicity or legal campaigns. The solutions in such cases usually involve attempts to establish national uniformity. But these attempts involve such great complexity at the level of administrative implementation that nonuniformities, often of particularly arbitrary and perverse kinds, frequently are introduced.[21]

New Approaches

The problems, implicit and explicit, identified throughout this book would not have persisted for some 200 years if they were easily handled. Indeed, it is fair to say that there are no perfect or complete solutions to these problems. Therefore, the suggestions below are offered tentatively and without illusions about their power to cure.

First, it does seem to me essential that the nation develop better ways of dealing with the short-run dislocations that follow from pecuniary externalities and from efforts to correct interstate (or for that matter, intrastate) spillovers. Making long-run policy to protect short-run interests is not an especially promising way to greet the future. While transfer payments and related programs are currently much in disfavor, the nation might well find that the real cost of even modestly inefficient transfers is less than that of maintaining inefficient pricing or pollution control or fisheries management policies into the indefinite future.[22]

More broadly, the country needs imaginative ways of compensating those people it asks (or orders) to bear some external cost as part of the solution to a regional conflict. As Kneese points out in chapter 4, water projects, military bases, and other facilities are traditional counters in this game. More to the point, and probably less costly, would be direct payments, especially if we could use modern ideas about demand revelation to provide an acceptable basis for choice of size.[23] Transfer payments are made as matters of policy to many groups other than welfare recipients. (Farmers, airlines, and local jurisdictions around large federal facilities come easily to mind.) It should not be beyond our collective wit to find ways to help directly those who may be harmed by a nuclear waste storage facility, for example, or by a limited-entry scheme for fisheries management.[24]

Second, new and more flexible definitions of "jurisdiction" could make it easier for affected interests to be heard. Thus, while place of residence might still be the desideratum for many or most issues, for some it might be possible to "contract into" a special nongeographic jurisdiction by agreeing in advance to help to pay the costs implied for others if one's view won out.[25] This might, for example, apply to decisions about preservation of certain natural areas, or to water projects, or to highway planning. Still, intervention in out-of-state disputes, whether through political campaigns or lobbying or litigating organizations, costs money, so such an innovation would have to be carefully structured to avoid problems raised by income limitations. But it need not be any less equitable than the current policy of "muddling through."

Finally, it also is worth reconsidering the potential place for and necessary structure of regional institutions. I am not optimistic, for the reasons spelled out above, but perhaps with a decentralizing administration eager to loosen Washington's strings and with a set of sufficiently juicy carrots with which to tempt the states to cede a little of their authority, legitimate and sufficiently powerful institutions could arise, for example, in the water resource field. But the carrots would have to include the power to raise money, not just a few years of easily withdrawn federal largesse, and real power to make decisions and distribute costs and benefits.

No government can guarantee happiness. It is enough—and decidedly more realistic—that ours enshrines its pursuit. Thus, a burden of my argument is that Americans stop trying to hold back the tide of most pecuniary externalities when the struggle involves disproportionate costs. Besides, not all such externalities are negative. Some are positive to start with and, as Rosenberg and Landsberg demonstrate at the outset, many seeming unpleasantries represent positive changes over the long run; still others tend to balance each other. Change is both natural and inevitable in any event. We should do what we can to ease transitions when action does not make matters worse, but to do more is both futile and needlessly costly.

Real and political externalities are better targets for collective concern and action. They can be more difficult than the "mere" pecuniary variety, and the sheer size, complexity, and productive power of modern society continually magnifies their difficulty. But they often can be ameliorated, if not eliminated, by creative and innovative approaches to building and changing the institutions that deal with them. As has been emphasized throughout this volume, adaptive change is a hallmark of the American experience.

Notes

1. I will for the most part follow Stewart in using regional conflict and interstate conflict interchangeably, primarily because regions lack decision-making institutions and thus are nothing but collections of states, with state decisions and actions defining "regional" positions.

2. See Tibor Scitovsky, "Two Concepts of External Cost," *Journal of Political Economy* vol. 62 (1954) pp. 143–151.

3. For an illuminating discussion, see Gary A. Miller, "Fragmentation and Inequality: The Politics of Metropolitan Organization," Ph.D. dissertation, The University of Texas at Austin, 1976.

4. This is not mere fanciful theory or let-them-eat-cake social policy. United Van Lines reports two telling statistics for the interstate household goods shipments it handled during 1981: for auto-depressed Michigan, 66 percent of the shipments were outbound; for oil-and-gas-rich Oklahoma, 62 percent were inbound—the highest such figure for any state (*The Wall Street Journal*, March 25, 1982, p. 1).

5. See U.S. Department of Energy, *Coal Data: A Reference*, Publication No. 061-003-00127-1 (Washington, D.C., GPO, July 1980).

6. Alaska proposes to return to residents one-half its "excess oil revenues" annually. This will be done in proportion to length of residence, a feature designed to limit the incentive for adjustment through mobility. This feature was challenged on equal protection grounds in the Alaskan courts (*Zobel* v. *Williams* 80-11-46), a challenge that was rebuffed by the Alaska Supreme Court (*The New York Times*, February 24, 1981). But just as this book went to press (June 1982), the Supreme Court ruled 8 to 1 against the state on the grounds that laws basing benefits on length of residence violate the Fourteenth Amendment guarantee of equal protection. Justice Brennan, in a concurring opinion, specifically pointed out that the Alaska law, if it were to stand, would place obstacles in the way of interstate mobility. Alaska has prepared an alternative position in which revenues will be returned to citizens on a flat per capita basis independent of length of residence.

7. It is not feasible fully to reproduce the arguments here. Briefly, physical externalities usually involve things or actions for which markets not only do not exist but for which they are difficult or impossible to institute. Where many "emitters" and many "receptors" are involved, the problems of *ad hoc* bargaining become very great and are exacerbated by the same features of the things or actions that make markets hard to establish. Central, collective decisions, with coercion to prevent "free riding" when it comes time to pay the bill, are usually seen as necessary. Some enthusiasts for markets would disagree. See, for example, Ronald Coase, "The Problem of Social Cost," *Journal of Law and Economics* vol. 3 (October 1960) pp. 1–44.

8. The Colorado River Compact, arrived at in 1922 with the help of a rather optimistic estimate of average annual flow, may be an important exception. See Kneese's discussion in chapter 4 and, for more extensive treatment, Allen V. Kneese and F. Lee Brown, The *Southwest Under Stress: National Resource Development Issues in a Regional Setting* (Baltimore, Md., The Johns Hopkins University Press for Resources for the Future, 1981).

9. Readers who wish to explore this idea in depth may profitably consult Allen V. Kneese and Blair T. Bower, *Managing Water Quality: Economics, Technology, Institutions* (Baltimore, Md., Johns Hopkins University Press for Resources for the Future, 1968);

and Daniel A. Okun, *Regionalization of Water Management* (London, Applied Science Publishers, 1977).

10. Kneese and Bower, *Managing Water Quality.*

11. Just to give a flavor of the air pollution problem, I offer our experience at Resources for the Future with an environmental quality model of the eleven-county lower Delaware River region. This region, only a subpart of the basin, is nonetheless useful for studying water quality management in the estuary. But it is less satisfactory as an air quality region. According to the EPA's emissions and ambient air quality inventory data, a fraction of total ambient sulfur dioxide concentrations in the region (somewhere between 5 and 50 percent depending on location) results from import across the regional boundaries from Maryland, farther west in Pennsylvania, and even the New York City region. The estimate of importation of suspended particulates is about 5 percent of ambient concentrations, but there remains considerable residual uncertainty expressed as a "calibration intercept" which amounts to about one half the National Ambient Air Quality Standard level of 75 micrograms per cubic meter for total suspended particulates.

12. The Fishery Conservation and Management Act of 1976 (P.L. 94-265) created regional fishery management councils with representation—indeed, control—for the coastal states in each of eight regions (including the waters of the Western Pacific around American Samoa and Guam). But, in fact, many important species range over several council areas. To cope with this, among other things, decisions of the councils are subject to veto at the national level by the secretary of commerce. See William R. Rogalski, "The Unique Federalism of the Regional Councils Under the Fishery Conservation and Management Act of 1976," *Environmental Affairs* vol. 9 (1980) pp. 163–203.

13. For examples of a range of regional government experiments, see Martha Derthick, *Between State and Nation: Regional Organizations of the United States* (Washington, D.C., The Brookings Institution, 1974).

14. Walter O. Spofford, Jr., Clifford S. Russell, and Robert A. Kelly, *Environmental Quality Management: Application to the Lower Delaware Valley* (Washington, D.C., Resources for the Future, 1976).

15. *New Jersey v. New York, et al.* 283 U.S. 336.1931. See also Roscoe C. Martin, *Water for New York* (Syracuse, N.Y., Syracuse University Press, 1960).

16. *The Wall Street Journal*, July 22, 1981, p. 12; and August 6, 1981, p. 28.

17. *The Los Angeles Times*, August 28, 1981, p. 1.

18. In the Clean Air Act, these procedures are explicitly spelled out in Section 126, "Interstate Air Pollution Abatement." The Clean Water Act does not contain such a tidy setting out of duties and procedures in the interstate context.

19. See *Inside EPA*, August 7, 1981, p. 8.

20. The especially vexing requirement is that the petitioning state show that achievement of the applicable NAAQS, prevention of significant deterioration, or visibility requirement "is prevented by named out-of-state sources" (see ibid., August 7, 1981, p. 7). On its face this seems to imply that a violation could be found only if all sources in the complaining state had reduced discharges to their lowest feasible limits and a violation still existed. No balancing of costs across state lines seems to be contemplated.

21. For example, the work of three of my colleagues on the EPA's administration of the water pollution control legislation reveals some striking differences in how industries and even parts of industries have been treated. See Henry Peskin, Winston Harrington, and Alan Krupnick, "Federal Rulemaking: A Statistical Analysis," draft report to the Alfred P. Sloan Foundation (Washington, D.C., Resources for the Future, May 1982).

22. For a useful and sobering discussion of compensation mechanisms, see Robert S. Goldfarb, "Compensating Victims of Policy Change," *Regulation* (September–October

1980) pp. 22–30. For more about trade adjustment, see Charles R. Frank, Jr., *Foreign Trade and Domestic Aid* (Washington, D.C., The Brookings Institution, 1977).

23. Two good sources on this topic are Edward Clarke, *Demand Revelation and the Provision of Public Goods* (Cambridge, Mass., Ballinger, 1980); and T. M. Tideman and G. Tullock, "A New and Superior Process for Making Social Choices," *Journal of Political Economy* vol. 84 (December 1976) pp. 1145–1159.

24. Again, see Goldfarb, "Compensating Victims."

25. Contracting into the fishery management decision process is a feature of the new Irish fishery management structure. See George Burrows, "The Irish Column," *Trout and Salmon* (October 1981) p. 14.

Epilogue

Gilbert F. White

The central focus of this book is on how people sharing moderately common aspirations and modes of political action deal in a variety of social situations with basic geographic disparities among places in resource endowment. Spatial differences in location, climate, water, soil, and minerals are inherent in any landscape. And because resources necessarily are defined jointly by their unique physical characteristics and the economic and technological conditions of their use, the boundaries of regions are shifting.

Fuzzy regional boundaries almost by definition delimit an area of potential friction, but disputes by no means are inevitable. For example, when regional differences are incorporated in a use system that recognizes comparative advantages and productive interchanges among unlike areas, as when dry grazing lands are linked with irrigated feed cropping to support an integrated livestock industry, they are harmonious. But when the uses work to regional disadvantage—as when coal mining in one area leads to its abandonment in another—conflicts arise. Indeed, regional development carries the seeds of dislocation of interregional links. Regional conflicts may fester for a long time without resolution, but they often become acute and attract attention in the wake of rapid changes in resource availability or technology or valuation of the kind that have profoundly shaped the course of energy production and use in the United States during the past decade. It is no coincidence that energy issues have dominated the examples presented in the previous chapters.

Our joint examination has three component questions. What are regional conflicts and how important are they to the life of the nation? What is the record of attempts to deal with them? What is the prospect for national policies that would respond to such conflicts more constructively?

Answers to these questions have been offered from the vantage of a variety of spokesmen only slightly fettered by disciplinary bounds. Economists have ventured judicial opinions. A legal scholar has discussed economic factors. An historian has summed up geography. And all have been willing to voice an opinion on political modalities.

Robert Kates has said that following a provocative exchange of this sort a well-intentioned mediator approached two participants entrenched in belligerent opposition. Taking one antagonist aside and listening to the argument, he concluded, "You are right, you are absolutely right." Then he heard the other's argument and decided, "You are right, you are absolutely right." An observer reminded the mediator he had taken a completely inconsistent position, to which he replied, after due deliberation, "You are right, you are absolutely right." Mediating the views presented in this volume runs the risk of taking such a posture, and it is encouraged by the evidence that some past conflicts have worked themselves out with the slow passage of time so that both sides to the debates at least were partly right.

What Are Regional Conflicts?

We deal first with notions of region and conflict. The contributors make it clear that the concept of region is ambiguous and may be applied in a variety of connotations. It may be taken to mean an area homogeneous in one respect, such as the dominance of cotton production, or the prevalence of warm winter temperatures, or the occurrence of coal beds. It may be used to describe an area that is functionally related among its parts, such as the basin drained by the Tennessee River system, or the "milkshed" sending farm products to a common market. For leg-islative and judicial purposes it simply may be an area under common political jurisdiction, usually a state or a cluster of states. In following public debates as well as these chapters, it is important to remember that the term is employed with different meanings.

An area defined as a region by one criterion may be highly hetero-geneous by other criteria. Colorado may be described as an energy-rich state, but it is also an assembly of plateaus rich in oil shale, pockets of petroleum production, Indian enclaves threatened or stressed by natural gas development, a large metropolitan area claiming West Slope waters, and an expanse of wheat- and corn-growing plains. There are as many tensions over resources within Colorado as between Colorado and other states.

Moreover, in the Denver area the vertical stress between low-income laborers and high-income energy property managers is as strong as that between irrigation farmers and synfuel entrepreneurs. To the array of colorful bumpersticker examples offered by my coauthors, I add one recently displayed on a Colorado pickup truck: "Out of work? Hungry? Eat an environmentalist!"

But what precisely is meant by "conflict?" Two classifications are presented, an economic definition of pecuniary, real, and political ex-ternalities by Russell, and a legal definition of legislative and judicial mechanisms by Stewart. The two in practice are much alike or, at least, are not inconsistent.

Rosenberg reminds us that regional conflicts always have been with us, and Landsberg and Kneese offer a range of contemporary issues that illustrate that the conditions of conflict are changing subtly and con-stantly. Technological innovation and international relations can alter the cast of characters and their roles.

Three factors seem to be new in the situation at the beginning of the 1980s. First, as suggested by each author and focused by Landsberg, the change in energy prices and availability has been revolutionary. It is too soon to draw any definitive conclusions—not even ten years have passed since the Arab oil embargo and subsequent OPEC price hike of 1973–74—but the evidence Landsberg presents surely is suggestive of major, long-lasting change.

Second, as Rosenberg shows, the United States is strongly affected by a rising concern for equity. This is reflected in egalitarian sensitivity to differences in economic income among regions and to prospective changes that would affect future generations. Per capita regional incomes may be converging, but many people seem to perceive the remaining differences all the more acutely and perception sometimes has a way of becoming reality.

Third, the goals of preserving and enhancing environmental quality have become enduring parts of the American scene. Ten years after the Stockholm Conference on the Human Environment the aims expressed there are shared by major publics in the United States, cutting across socioeconomic lines. As a result, the environmental impact of technological changes is a legitimate target of public appraisal, much more so than in any previous period of regional conflict.

Energy, equity, and environment have changed the framework of regional debate, and have increased the importance of resource analysis in advancing it.

The Record of Collective Decision Making

Either explicitly or implicitly, each contributor to this exploration has seen conflict as an essential ingredient of organic growth: what is true of a cell or an organism is true of a nation. And each offers evidence that the links among parts of the nation have been changing, always with effects upon their relative roles. The statistics on population redistribution, real energy costs, and narrowing per capita income differentials are impressive. But there is less evidence about the consequences of collective attempts to respond to changing conditions.

As a part of the mediation of stresses and shifts that now favor one area and now another, the nation has engaged in a long maneuver of income transfers to somehow restore equity among the regions. Public land grants for railroads, irrigation subsidies, soil conservation assistance, and severance taxes are only a few. The policies were plain; the resulting changes in income, if any, remain in doubt.

How do we sort out the effects of these past and present transfer efforts? They are so deep and pervasive that any attempt to determine the causes of present conflict leads almost invariably to earlier corrective action. Indeed, as Kneese points out in the case of increasing salinity in the Colorado River, the recent problem had its roots in a 1944 treaty with Mexico that ignored the question of water quality. That treaty in turn was preceded by the 1922 Colorado River Compact which, in addition to overallocating the normal flow of the river, also said nothing about quality. Nor does Kneese's review of the present corrective action give any cause for optimism. Despite a shift of hefty regional costs to the nation at large, he predicts the issue will rise again.

Solutions that do not solve, corrective actions that often end up making things worse, indecision and institutional buckpassing—the record of collective decision making is checkered at best, and one is inclined to applaud loudly when Stewart and Russell call for new approaches and institutions to deal with regional disputes.

National Policy Prospects

Still, however—and perhaps surprisingly—the general position that emerges from these analyses is benign. It might have been otherwise if an ardent state protagonist, say, or an environmental activist had contributed, but the authors nonetheless are persuasive that, given time and prudent selection of measures, regional conflicts need not become deeply divisive or disruptive.

Essentially, the choice of actions is between market adjustments or government guidance as expressed in either regulations or subsidies. Ironically, however, both laissez-faire and the two types of governmental activity may get in the way of those shifts in process that may turn out to be in the public interest. Forecasting the future never will be an exact science. Historically, the market has worked well over the long term, if at occasional short-term cost. But the market does fail, and environmental pollution is a classic example. The range of possible actions to circumvent market failure embraces the device of side payments, measures to ease real and pecuniary dislocations, increases in jurisdictional flexibility, and decentralized administration and incentive programs. In due course, some combination of these may help resolve regional inequities without serious harm to national well-being.

It has become a cliché in a volume of this sort to announce that more research is needed. Still, I must point out that the opportunities for research to clarify the options for dealing with regional conflict are large. The roots of conflict must be elucidated. Alternative responses must be more carefully evaluated. And the perceptions of these roots and responses must be probed so that people working on policy may be aware of how the conditions and choices are viewed by others involved.

In a review of the state of the global environment during the last decade I was impressed by the simple axiom that without social and political stability, the efficacy of any national corrective measure for environmental disruption is moot. The same constraint applies to appraising national options: the national choice will be affected strongly by the state of the economy and the integrity of the political leadership.

Looking ahead, it may well be that international considerations will strongly shape the course of actions taken within the United States. Just as the North American migratory waterfowl treaty spurred domestic wildlife preservation programs, recognition of national obligations for controlling carbon dioxide and sulfur dioxide emissions, as they may affect world climate and ecosystem health, may shape the energy policy measures the United States takes as a nation. Similarly, considerations of the world supply of foodstuffs may influence the choice of actions taken to preserve soils and rangeland vegetation. In those and other circumstances a world view may lead to subordinating regional inequity to national interest. But that is a subject for another forum and another book.

About the Contributors

Emery N. Castle is president and senior fellow at Resources for the Future. He came to RFF in 1976 from Oregon State University, where he had been professor and head of the Department of Agricultural Economics, dean of faculty, and dean of the Graduate School. He has been president of the American Agricultural Economics Association and chairman of Oregon's Water Policy Review Board, among other public and professional duties. He is co-editor of *U.S.–Japanese Agricultural Trade Relations*, published by RFF in 1982.

Allen V. Kneese is a senior fellow in the Quality of the Environment Division at Resources for the Future; he formerly was director of the division and of RFF's water resource program. He has taught resource economics at the Universities of New Mexico, California, and Michigan, and at Stanford University. He has been a consultant to many national and international organizations and has published widely in the fields of natural resources and the environment. He is co-editor of two recent RFF books, *The Southwest Under Stress: National Resource Development Issues in a Regional Setting,* and *Environmental Regulation and the U.S. Economy,* both published in 1981.

Hans H. Landsberg is a senior fellow and former director of the Center for Energy Policy Research at Resources for the Future. He joined RFF in 1960, was coauthor of one of its first major publications, *Resources in America's Future* (1963), and directed its programs of resource appraisals and of energy and materials. A consultant to many governmental and nongovernmental organizations, he was chairman of the Ford Foundation-sponsored study group that produced *Energy: The Next Twenty Years* (1979). He is coauthor of *High Energy Costs: Uneven, Unfair, Unavoidable?*, published for RFF in 1981.

Kent A. Price is associate director of public affairs and assistant to the president at Resources for the Future. He is the principal writer and editor of RFF's *Annual Report* and other institutional materials, co-editor of its quarterly, *Resources*, and was a contributor to the silver anniversary volume, *Resources for the Future: The First Twenty-Five Years* (1977). Before joining RFF in 1975, he was chief writer for the president of the University of California.

Nathan Rosenberg is Fairleigh S. Dickinson, Jr., Professor of Public Policy in the Department of Economics at Stanford University. A former member of the faculties at Indiana and Purdue Universities and at the Universities of Pennsylvania and Wisconsin, his many published articles and books include *Technology and American Economic Growth* (1972), *Perspectives on Technology* (1976), and *The Britannia Bridge: The Generation and Diffusion of Technological Knowledge* (1978).

Clifford S. Russell is director and senior fellow of the Quality of the Environment Division at Resources for the Future. At RFF since 1968, he has concentrated on the analysis of environmental problems, including the costs and benefits of pollution control, institutions for making public decisions about environmental quality, and alternative ways of translating decisions into actions. He has published many books and articles and has edited volumes of collected papers on these themes, most recently *Public Choice and Rural Development* (1981). He has taught resource economics at The Johns Hopkins University and the University of Maryland and has served on committees of the National Academy of Sciences, the Organisation for Economic Co-Operation and Development, and the American Water Works Association.

Richard B. Stewart is a professor of law at the Harvard Law School, which he joined in 1971. He specializes in administrative and regulatory law, and is the coauthor of *Administrative Law and Regulatory Policy* (1978) and *Environmental Law and Policy* (Second Edition, 1978), among other scholarly publications. He has served as a Supreme Court law clerk and special counsel to the Senate Watergate Committee, and currently is chairman of the Board of Trustees of the Environmental Defense Fund.

Paul E. Tsongas is the junior U.S. Senator from Massachusetts. A Democrat, he was elected to the Senate in 1978 following two terms in the House of Representatives. His committee assignments include Small Business; Foreign Relations, to which he brings experience as a former volunteer and staff member of the Peace Corps; and, of particular relevance to this volume, Energy and Natural Resources. He is the author of *The Road from Here: Liberalism and Realities in the 1980s* (1981).

Gilbert F. White is a geographer and former director of the Institute of Behavioral Science at the University of Colorado at Boulder. He has been a member of the faculty at the University of Chicago, president of Haverford College, chairman of RFF's Board of Directors, and in various capacities has served the federal government, nonprofit organizations, the United Nations and other international agencies, and the National Academy of Sciences and the National Research Council. His studies of natural resources began during the New Deal with service for the Mississippi Valley Committee of the Public Works Administration and continued with work on water resources, arid lands, and natural hazards in the United States and overseas. His most recent book, which he co-edited, is *The World Environment, 1972–1982*.

Index

Acid rain, 10, 88, 102, 119
Ackerman, Bruce A. 37
Agriculture: adjustment process in, 26; cyclic nature of, 6; expansion in, 26; federal policy on, 26; productivity growth in, 25; railroads and, 25; refrigeration and, 25; regional convergence in, 26; in regional development, 6; results of specialization in, 26
Air pollution: Reagan administration and, 119; as source of regional conflict, 35
Air quality, 35
American history, 15, 19
Appalachia, 68
Arab oil embargo, 18
Articles of Confederation: abandonment of, 4; as basis of modern institutions, 10; foreign trade under, 89; internal trade under, 89; interstate conflicts under, 89; regional conflicts under, 4; retaliatory tariffs under, 89; state barriers and, 89
Atomic Energy Act, 100
Atomic Energy Commission, 77

Baucus, Sen. Max (D-Mont.), 68–69, 72
Bingaman, Jeff, 76

Boston Edison, 39
Boundaries, 1–2
Brennan, Justice William, 123
Brown, F. Lee, 70, 71
Brownell, Herbert, Jr., 61, 62, 63
Bryce Canyon National Park, 103
Burciaga, U.S. District Judge Juan, 80
Burlington Northern Railroad, 39
Byrne, Gov. Brendan, 58

Cape Cod, 99
Carter, President Jimmy, 38, 100
Central Arizona Project, 67
Central Utah Project, 67
Champlain, Lake, 118
Civil War, 4; and doctrine of nullification, 20; impact of on income, 27; regional domination as issue in, 19. *See also* Regional conflict.
Clean Air Act of 1970, 22, 35; and acid rain, 102; "continuous cleaning" provision of, 36–37; emissions regulations in, 36; environmentalist support for, 37; 1977 revision of, 36; purpose of, 119; results of, 38; as source of regional conflict, 37–38
Clean Coal/Dirty Air, 37

Clean Water Act, 22, 117, 119
Coachella Canal, 62
Coal: as nonrenewable resource, 68, 97; transportation of, 39–40
Coal slurry pipelines: arguments for, 39; Congress and, 39; Energy Department and, 39; loss of water in, 38, 39; opponents to, 39; opposition to, 38–39; prevention of, 38; as source of regional conflict, 38–40; supporters of, 39
Collective decision-making, 129–30
Colorado Basin, 60
Colorado Basin Project Act, 64
Colorado River Basin Salinity Program, 64
Colorado River Compact of 1922, 61, 129
Colorado River: international treaty on, 8; salinity of, 8, 59, 60–67; treaty of 1944, 61
Colorado River Salinity Control Program, 62
Colorado River salinity: Congress and, 62; effect of on Mexico, 61; Glen Canyon Dam and, 61; inevitability of increases in, 66; international agreement on, 63; as international issue, 61; National Academy of Sciences and, 64; negotiations with Mexico about, 61–62; Nixon administration and, 61–62; as pecuniary externality, 59; permissible absolute levels of, 66; as real externality, 59; reduction of as national obligation, 64; as source of regional conflict, 8, 87; Wellton-Mohawk Project and, 61
Colorado River salinity agreement: as distributive politics, 67; extraneous considerations in, 65; factors in, 65–66; means of implementing, 66; reasons for, 64–66
Columbia River treaty, 65
Commerce Clause: claims under, 70–71; congressional authority under, 91, 99; federal courts' initiatives under, 92; judicial invocation of, 91; Montana coal tax case and, 69–70; and restriction of interstate commerce, 91; state powers under, 95
Commerce power: origin of, 90; congressional exercise of, 98–99
Commercial nuclear wastes, 77
Commonwealth Edison, et al. v. Montana, et al., 69, 71, 94
Compact Clause. See U.S. Constitution
Complete Auto Transit, Inc. v. Brady, 71
Compromise of 1850, 19
Conflict: as contributor to organic growth, 129; economic definition of, 128; legal definition of, 128
Congress: commerce power of, 98; delegation of power by, 99; preemptive powers of, 99–101; regulatory powers of, 9, 90, 99
Consumer Price Index, 55

Cooke, Alistair, 5
Corn Belt, 24
Cotton: Belt, 24; cultivation of, 25

Delaware River Basin Committee, 117
Detroit Edison Company, 73
Devolution, philosophy of, 69
Distributive politics: Colorado River salinity agreement as, 67; interbasin water transfers as, 67; and western water, 63
Durenberger, Sen. David F. (IR-Minn.), 69, 73, 74
Dumars, Charles, 70, 71
Dynamic force, 29

Economic activity: market interactions and, 10; regional distribution of, 15, 31; side effects of, 22; pecuniary externalities and, 113
Economic growth: and regional distributional shifts, 31; regional specialization and, 24; technological change and, 30
Economic rents, 60
Edgar, Rep. Robert W. (D-Pa.), 117 n.4
Egalitarian ethic, 21
Electricity prices: hydroelectricity and, 55; nuclear power and, 55; in TVA area, 56
Energy: availability of, 34; commodities, 13; consumption pattern, 54; distribution of, 49; price of, 34, 41; problem, 40; production of, 35; regional statistics on, 54–55; resources, 45; shortages of, 34; as source of regional conflict, 5, 12, 35
Energy-deficient states: per capita income in, 47, fig. 3–3; population movement from, 45; severance taxes and, 42–43; uneven burden on, 40
Energy, Department of: coal slurry pipelines and, 39; consumer survey by, 51; and licensing for WIPP, 78; negotiations of with New Mexico, 79; New Mexico complaint against, 9, 76, 78–84; as replacement for ERDA; vacillation of, 78; WIPP court order and, 80
Energy expenditures: per household, 54, table 3–7; range of, 54–55; regional differences in, 54, table 3–7; state-by-state differences in, 54
Energy Mobilization Board, 100
Energy prices: for bottled gas, 52; differentials in at user level, 52; distributional aspects of, 46; effect of on consumers, 49; effect of on employment, 46; effect of on income, 46; for electricity, 51; and energy endowment, 49; for fuel oil and kerosene, 51; gradual increase of, 53; inadequacy of snapshot approach to, 53; for natural gas, 51; quantity

consumed as factor in, 52; regional averages of, 52, table 3–6; regional variations in, 51, table 3–5

Energy Research and Development Adminstration (ERDA), 78

Energy-surplus states: congressional voting strength of, 47; growth rates of, 47; location of, 47; price differentials and, 52; shift of employment to, 40; shift of income to, 40

Environment: conflict about, 10–11, 12; degradation of, 97; equity and, 22; federal policies on, 22; preservation of, 103; quality of life and, 22

Environmental Protection Agency, 22, 37, 99, 119

Equity: as source of regional conflict, 12

Erie Canal, 25

Externalities: concept of, 10; definition of, 59, 111; geographical jurisdictional system and, 112; in resource conflicts, 112; as source of regional conflict, 59, 111

Fair Labor Standards Act, 82

Federal courts: review by of federal actions, 79, 80; responsibility of to delimit congressional powers, 100; role of in regional conflict, 10, 87, 88; and state regulation of interstate commerce, 92

Federal government: regional domination of, 19; responsibility of, 15

Federalist, The, 89, 90

Federal Land Policy and Management Act of 1976 (FLPMA), 79–80, 81

Federal Mineral Leasing Act, 100

Federal system: compromises of perpetuating, 19; operation of, 88; and regional conflict, 88–89; westward movement and, 19

Federal Water Pollution Act of 1972, 102

Free Wendland, Republic of, 75

Friends of the Earth, 39

Frontier thesis, 19

Forum on Regional Conflict and National Policy, 11

Fox, Irving, 66

Garreau, Joel, 17 n.1

General Accounting Office, 78

Georges Bank, 99

Gerry, Elbridge, 89

Gillette, Wyoming, 2, 38

Glen Canyon Dam, 61

Gorleben, West Germany, 75

Gorsuch, Anne, 119

Great Depression: equity concerns and, 6, 21; impact of on income distribution, 21; and modern welfare state, 20

Growth rates: disparity in, 29; indicators of, 26

Hamilton, Alexander, 90

Hassler, William T., 37

Heisler v. Thomas Colliery, 70, 71

High-level nuclear wastes: characteristics of, 76; commercial, 76; definition of, 75; military, 78

Hoch, Irving, 54

House Armed Services Committee, 78

Hydroelectricity, 55

Illinois v. Milwaukee, 101–102, 118, 119

Imperial Dam, 66

Imperial Valley, California, 60

Income: Civil War and, 27; differentials in, 27; distribution of, 6; national per capita, 27, table 2–1; regional convergence of, 28; regional per capita, 28, table 2–2; tax on, 20

Interior, Department of, 80, 81, 99

International agreements: internal forces affecting, 66; on river problems, 64–66

International Paper Company, 118

International Water and Boundary Commission, 62

Interstate commerce: congressional oversight of, 91; congressional regulation of, 89; constitutional regulation of, 89; discriminatory burdens on, 93–94; early court decisions on, 91; federal judiciary and, 89, 91; legal definition of, 91; legitimate state interest in, 91; natural resource taxes and, 93; nondiscriminatory burdens on, 94–95; as source of regional conflict, 90–91; state and local taxes on, 9, 92; state-imposed burdens on, 90–91; states' regulation of, 92

Interstate resource conflicts: congressional powers in, 89, 98–101; development of new institutions for, 104–105; environmental protection as issue in, 97; federal system and, 88; judicial retreat from, 88, 95–98; legal process and, 87, 88; nonmarket values of, 97; pecuniary externalities and, 114, 115–16; role of judiciary in, 105; scenic values as source of, 103; statutory ambiguity and, 99–100; Supreme Court rulings on, 93–95; technical complexity of, 96; transboundary pollution as, 88, 101–104

Interstate spillover conflicts: congressional regulations and, 102; judicial deference in, 102–103; sewage discharge as, 101

Izaak Walton League, 39

Jackson, Mr. Justice, 92
Jicarilla Apache tribe, 75

Kansas-Nebraska Act of 1854, 19
Kates, Robert, 127
Kneese, Allen V., 8–9, 97, 104, 117, 121, 128, 129, 130
Krutilla, John V., 65

Land Management, Bureau of, 80, 81
Landsberg, Hans H., 4, 6–7, 122, 128
Lee, Robert E., 2
Leman, Christopher K., 5, 13
Leven, Charles, 45
Los Alamos National Laboratory, 76
Los Medanos, 76, 77
Love Canal, 31
Low-Level Radioactive Waste Policy Act of 1980, 105

Malthus, John, 30
Mann, Dean, 63
Maryland v. Louisiana, 93–94
Mason, George, 2
Mexicali Valley, 66
Mexican-Americans, 14
Miernyk, William, 46
Military transuranic wastes, 77, 78
Minerals Land Leasing Act of 1920, 72
Mining: costs of, 68, 72; environmental controls on, 93; environmental damage by, 68; social damage of, 68
Minnesota v. Cloverleaf Diary, 95
Minute 242, 62
Missouri Compromise of 1820, 19
Missouri-Mississippi River systems, 67
Montana coal tax, 13; as appropriation of economic rent, 67; basis of court case on, 69–70; constitutionality of, 71–72; controversiality of, 8–9, 68–69; as environmental protection measure, 98; and interstate commerce, 71; issues in court case on, 69; level of, 9, 68; as pecuniary externality, 114; as source of regional conflict, 8–9, 87; state revenues and, 69; Supreme Court ruling on, 9, 68, 69–72; technical complexity of, 96

National Academy of Sciences, 41, 64
National Ambient Air Quality Standard, 119
National Coal Association, 39
National Coal Policy Project, 38
National Energy Plan (1977), 38

National Environmental Policy Act of 1969 (NEPA), 79, 80–81
National League of Cities v. Usery, 82, 84
Natural gas, 56
Natural resources: Commerce Clause and, 92, 93; cost of developing, 68; economic performance and, 30; market impacts of, 93; regional income and, 30; regulation and taxation of, 92–95; as source of regional conflict, 4, 88; systemic regional character of, 96
Navaho Indians, 31
New Frontier, 16
New Mexico: acceptance by of nuclear waste, 78; complaint of against DOE, 76–84; concurrence rights of, 78; negotiations of with DOE, 79; nuclear waste storage in, 76, 77, 78; role of in WIPP, 78
New Mexico complaint: basis of, 80–81; causes of, 78–79; court order on, 80; issues in, 79–80; FLPMA violation as issue in, 81; land withdrawal as issue in, 81; NEPA violation as issue in, 81; states' rights as issue in, 60, 80, 81, 82–84; Tenth Amendment as basis of, 60
Nixon, Richard M., 61
North American Water and Power Alliance, 67
Northeast-Midwest Institute, 41, 51
Northeast-Midwest Congressional Coalition, 41, 56
Nuclear Regulatory Commission, 78
Nuclear wastes: definition of, 75–76; plutonium as, 77; as source of regional conflict, 9; sources of, 76; storage of, 75–77 passim
Nuclear waste storage: Atomic Energy Commission and, 77; constitutionality of, 76; danger of, 77; problem of, 75–76; protests against, 75; temporary, 76; use of salt deposits for, 76–77
Nullification, doctrine of, 20

Occupational Safety and Health Administration, 22
Oil price decontrol, 41
Organization of Petroleum Exporting Countries (OPEC), 34, 51, 128
Outer Continental Shelf, 93

Pacific Gas and Electric, 39
Pecuniary externalities: adjustments to, 113; Colorado River salinity as, 59; compensation for, 121; definition of, 10–11, 111; as economic rents, 114–15; market interactions as, 10; new approaches to, 121; and potential state monopoly, 115; reactions to, 113-14; regional income differentials and, 116; short-

run problems and, 115; severance taxes as, 114; as signals in market economy, 113; state policies and, 114

Per capita income: and cost of energy, 46; in energy-deficient states, 47, fig. 3–3; in energy-surplus states, 47, fig. 3–3; as percentage of national average, 48, fig. 3–2; shifts in, 46–50

Plutonium, 77

Political externalities: consequences of, 120; definition of, 11, 111; examples of, 111; mechanisms for managing, 11, 119–20; as source of regional conflict, 111

Population: centers of, fig. 3–1; movement of, 28, 45, 49, 113

Population growth: and energy endowment, 45; regional patterns in, 45, table 3–4; westward shift, 7, 13

Population shifts: and energy distribution, 49; pecuniary externalities and, 113; reasons for, 28; westward, 7, 13

Public Law 996–164, 79 (see also, Waste Isolation Pilot Project)

Reagan, President Ronald W., 69

Reagan administration, 119

Real externalities: Colorado River salinity as, 59; definition of, 111; economic view of, 116; examples of, 111; interstate conflicts over, 119; pollution as, 119; resolution of conflicts about, 117; social management of, 11; as source of regional conflict, 116–17; state policies as, 11

Reclamation, Bureau of, 61

Regional conflict: air pollution as, 35; awareness of, 18; and Articles of Confederation, 4, 89; Civil War and, 4; collective institutions and, 110; commerce as source of, 89; compensation as solution to, 121; concepts of, 127–28; constitutional convention and, 89; definition of, 4; distinguishing factors of, 12; development as source of, 126; and energy crisis, 6; economic, 20, 24–26; energy as source of, 35; equity considerations in, 21; externalities and, 59; federal income tax and, 20; freedom of states as source of, 88; future of, 7, 130; historical context of, 4, 12, 18–20; inevitability of, 5; and institutional inadequacy, 9; interstate commerce as source of, 90–91; legal process and, 87, 118–19; and nationalism, 14; national policy prospects for, 130–31; natural resources and, 4, 8–9, 30, 88, 92–95, 96; new factors in, 128–29; news media and, 12, 18; options for dealing with, 130; pecuniary externalities and, 59, 114, 116; po-

litical externalities and, 111; real externalities and, 116–17, 119; during Reconstruction, 4; redefining jurisdiction as solution to, 121; role of federal courts in, 87; sources of, 4, 5, 6, 7, 13, 22, 57; transportation costs and, 24–26; toxic waste as source of, 104; uneven energy distribution and, 40; U. S. Constitution and, 90; volatile nature of, 126–27; western preponderance of, 1, 13

Regional development: agriculture and, 6; historical context of, 23; as source of conflict, 126

Regional income differentials: dynamic forces and, 29; national policies and, 21; pecuniary externalities and, 116; perceptions of inequity in, 31

Regional institutions: constitutional infirmities of, 117; as creatures of interstate treaties, 117; desirability of, 121; encouragement of, 117; examples of, 117; lack of power in, 118; problems of definition, 117

Regions: boundaries of, 126; concept of, 127; and congressional voting behavior, 20; convergence of income in, 28; definition of, 21; demographic trends in, 28; diversity of, 30; equity among, 6, 21, 30, 129; growth of, 6, 14; legal existence of, 3; management of, 14–16; movement among, 27; notion of, 2, 3; problems of defining; 128; specialization in, 24, 25; welfare of, 15

Regions, Resources, and Economic Growth, 15

Resources: conflicts about, 4, 8–9, 10–11, 18–19, 30, 88, 92–95, 96; discovery of, 29–30; needs for, 30

Resources for the Future, 3, 5, 11

Revenue-sharing, 43, 44

Rhine River salinity, 64–65

Rosenberg, Nathan, 4, 5–6, 122, 128

Russell, Clifford S., 3, 10–11, 14, 128, 130

Sagebrush Rebellion, 1, 14, 18

Salinity, 8, 59, 60–61, 64–65, 88

Sandia Laboratory, 76, 77

San Francisco Bay Area, 2

Severance taxes: application of, 72; attempts to limit, 42–43, 72–73; on coal, 68; comparative levels of, 68; congressional action on, 72–74; controversy over, 43–44; as example of economic rent, 60; and federal financial aid, 43; on federal lands, 68, 72; hostility to, 57; implications of proposed legislation for, 73–74; interstate commerce and, 72; Jicarilla Apache case, 75; and law of supply and demand, 44; legality of, 72; market impacts of, 93; on oil and natural gas, 68; opposition to, 4; as pecu-

Severance Taxes (continued)
niary externalities, 114; as percentage of
gross value, 41, table 3–2; as percentage of
state revenue, 41, table 3–3; proposed legislation on, 73; relationship of to state revenues,
41; reaction of energy-deficient states to, 42–
43; responses to, 44; right of states to levy,
69; as source of regional conflict, 7, 8–9, 13;
Supreme Court ruling on, 68, 69–72, 74–75;
technical complexity of, 96; use of for trust
funds, 72–73. See also Montana coal tax.
Site and Preliminary Design Validation Pro-
gram, 81
Smithsonian Institution, 5
Snake River, 67
Snowbelt vs. Sunbelt, 5, 7, 13, 18, 21, 50
Social Security, 21
Southern Pacific Railroad, 39
Southwest water politics, 63
State Energy Data Report, 51
States' rights, 18, 60, 80, 81, 82–84
Stewart, Richard B., 3, 9–10, 110–11, 117, 118,
119, 123, 128, 130
Stockholm Conference on the Human Environ-
ment, 129
Supremacy Clause. See U. S. Constitution
Supreme Court. See U.S. Supreme Court

Tauke, Rep. Tom (R-Iowa), 68, 72
Technological change: as balancing factor, 29;
as dynamic force, 29; economic growth and,
30; effects of, 30–31; function of, 30
Tehachapi Mountains, 2
Tennessee Valley Authority, 56
Tenth Amendment, 9, 60, 82–84. See also New
Mexico complaint; States' rights
Three Mile Island, 77
Tobacco Belt, 24
Toxic Substances Control Act, 22
Toxic waste: congressional regulation of, 103;
disposal of, 103–104; as source of regional
conflict, 104
Transportation, Department of, 39
Transuranic waste: as commercial byproduct,

77; definition of, 76; military, 77, 78; storage
of, 77, 78
Turner, Frederick Jackson, 19

United Mine Workers, 35, 39
U. S. Constitution: Commerce Clause of, 69–
71, 91, 92, 95, 99; Compact Clause of, 90; interstate commerce regulation in, 89; and regional conflict, 90; Supremacy Clause of, 69,
71, 72, 99
U. S. House of Representatives, 36, 78
U. S. Supreme Court: as arbiter of regional
conflict, 87–88; deference of, 95–98; establishment of, 89; in Illinois sewage case, 101–
102; in interstate resource conflicts, 93–95; in
Jicarilla Apache case, 75; jurisdiction of, 89–
90; in Montana coal tax, 9, 68, 69–72; and
severance taxes, 68, 69–72, 74–75

Vermont v. New York, 118
"Victim-pays" agreements, 64

Washington, George, 2
Waste Isolation Pilot Project (WIPP): authorizing legislation for, 77, 79, 82–83; Bureau of
Land Management and, 80, 81; congressional
intent for, 83; constitutionality of, 79; as
demonstration project, 78; as example of regional conflict, 87; federal court order on, 80;
final disposition of, 84; funding for, 78; Inte-
rior Department and, 80, 81; licensing of, 78;
Los Medanos as site of, 77; nature and scope
of, 77–78; Record of Decision on, 79; rela-
tionship of to national defense, 82, 83; as research and development facility, 78; role of
New Mexico in, 78; suitability of, 84; as
Tenth Amendment states' rights issue, 60
Wellton-Mohawk Project, 61, 62
Western coal, 35–36, table 3–1
Wheat Belt, 24
White, Gilbert F., 11–12, 15
Whitney, Eli, 25